Guardians of Churchill's Secret Army

MEN OF THE INTELLIGENCE CORPS
IN THE
SPECIAL OPERATIONS EXECUTIVE

Peter Dixon

Cloudshill Press

Cheltenham and London, England

Published by **Cloudshill Press LLP**

Registered Office: 27 Old Gloucester Street, London WC1N 3AX United Kingdom

Book Layout ©2015 BookDesignTemplates.com

Ordering Information:

Quantity sales: special discounts are available on quantity purchases by corporations, associations and others. For details, contact the publisher at the address above.

Guardians of Churchill 's Secret Army / Peter Dixon. -- 1st ed.

ISBN 978-0-9935080-3-5

Contents

For Miles, Emily, Leo, Julia and Henry

A new generation in a perplexing world

Preface

IN APRIL 1943, AGENT STOCKBROKER of the Special Operations Executive parachuted into a moonlit field in German-occupied France. Despite several close shaves, he succeeded in his clandestine mission, remained free and survived the war. Two months later, Agent *Valentin* too descended by night under a silk canopy, to a different part of France. Just days later, he was captured and eventually executed. In the following year, a month after D-Day, Agent *Adjacent* dropped with six comrades into the hilly Haute Vienne region of southwest France to support French Resistance fighters in their attempt to hinder German reinforcements.

These three brave men – and many more like them – risked their lives to fulfil Winston Churchill's 1940 order to 'Set Europe Ablaze'. Some of these agents survived. Many did not. But it was not just a matter of luck. As important were the suspicion and caution with which they approached undercover life and the tricks they had learned to keep themselves secure.

This book tells the mostly unknown human stories of the small group of men – yes, they were all men – who were brought into SOE, straight from Intelligence Corps training, to keep the organisation secure. They were junior in rank, but far from ordinary people. They were Australian, Anglo-French, Canadian, Scandinavian, East European and British. They had been schoolteachers, journalists, artists, ship brokers, racehorse trainers and international businessmen. Each spoke several languages. Their contribution has not yet been fully recognised.

Their initial role was 'Field Security' and started out as ensuring the security of agents about to be deployed on hazardous missions. Trained in counter-intelligence and skilled in a range of foreign languages, they could get alongside men and women who were preparing to risk their lives in France, Norway, Belgium and further afield. Many – like the three I have mentioned above – developed a much more active role themselves, in SOE operations worldwide.

The subjects of this book were almost exclusively men. Although women served in support of the Intelligence Corps – many in the Auxiliary Territorial Service – its personnel were all male. Thus women, who were such an important part of SOE, regrettably do not get much of a look-in here. This may be thought imbalanced, but books and even films about SOE heroines abound. *Carve Her Name with Pride*, the story of Violette Szabo, is one.

This is by no means the first book about the Special Operations Executive, the organisation tasked by Winston Churchill in 1940 to take the fight to the enemy, when desperately weakened Britain had few options. Without trying hard, I found 290 such books in English. Exciting narratives have revealed the heroic operations of the men and women parachuted into Nazi-occupied territory: wreaking havoc and encouraging, supporting and coordinating the efforts of those brave enough to resist harsh and brutal regimes. Academic historians have pored over sparse documentation to work out how great a role SOE – and the Resistance movements with which it worked – played in the Allied war effort. The disputes, too, have been documented: between SOE and the Secret Intelligence Service (SIS); between SOE and the more conventional military commanders and political leaders in London; between rival political factions – in France, in Belgium, in Greece – over money and weapons; and between Allies.

By describing the activities and the global reach of the Intelligence Corp's Field Security men in SOE, I aim to fill a substantial gap in the history of the Second World War for the non-specialist reader, between histories of the two organisations. The Intelligence Corps has been less comprehensively documented than SOE, but good histories exist, such as *Sharing the Secret* by Nicholas Van der Bijl, who devotes a chapter to SOE.

I am not alone in trying to fill this gap in the history; Christopher Murphy's *Security and Special Operations* is a fine academic study of SOE's security, particularly its relations with MI5,[1] between 1939 and 1945. However, my aim is different. I focus on the personal fates of the thirty-eight men who, with their Field Security Officers, were members of the first three Field Security Sections (63, 64 and 65 FSS) formed in January and February 1941 to support SOE. Their families contribute to the narrative. So too do some of the more than 100 Field Security men who subsequently joined the organisation, where their stories help to build the overall picture.

Even this cannot possibly be the whole story, though. About 600 Intelligence Corps officers and NCOs, including these Field Security men, served with SOE world-wide. This was about a tenth of the Corps' wartime strength; they worked as staff officers, country section heads, security staff, planners and instructors. A number of them operated behind enemy lines in Europe, the Middle East and the Far East. Much has been written on the more senior of them, rather less on the Field Security personnel, who were often not seen as 'important'. My focus is on relatively junior individuals, rather than the personal rivalries of politicians or the inevitable disputes between departments. In secret Whitehall, battles raged. Winston Churchill

---

[1] Although the term 'Security Service' is more accurate, particularly today, I use the more widely understood term 'MI5'. In contrast, the Secret Intelligence Service is today more openly known under that name rather than as MI6, so I use 'SIS'.

was frequently SOE's saviour. He was determined that SOE or something like it should exist. For these political aspects of SOE's history or to trace loose ends, readers can find plenty in the Note on Sources to satisfy their curiosity.

This book, then, is about the relationship between SOE's secret agents and the men who tried to keep them secure and safe. But many of those guardians became courageous agents themselves. Also, they were secret agents, but not spies. Although they often delivered intelligence to the right quarters, SOE's role was not meant to be espionage. These brave men and women went undercover in occupied Europe and elsewhere to implement Churchill's vision of irregular warfare, something we will discover as the book progresses.

I start us on this journey by looking at a man who deserves more attention than he has had. His wartime career illustrates the spirit of SOE's people, emphasises how important training was to the organisation and shows that in some cases survival depended very much on luck. His progress encapsulates in microcosm much of what I explore in the rest of the book. His name was Teddy Bisset.

CHAPTER 1

One Man's War

'*Never yield to force. Never yield to the apparently overwhelming might of the enemy.*'
Winston Churchill, speech at Harrow School,
29th October 1941

Teddy Bisset in Paris, 1939

Teddy Bisset

TEDDY BISSET WAS BORN IN PARIS in October 1915 to a French mother and a British father. These were the early years of the Great War, when enthusiasm for fighting the 'war to end all wars' was still high. Nearly thirty years later, it was Teddy's fluency in French and English that brought him back to France to fight secretly and heroically in a second global conflict. Through Teddy's story, we gain our first insight into the relationship between the people of the Intelligence Corps and the Special Operations Executive.

Teddy's father Alfred was a Scottish banker who was working in France during the First World War. He met and married Renée Marie Lacroix in 1915 and appears to have stayed in France after the war. He died in Normandy in 1934 at the age of 51. The widowed Renée and Teddy stayed in France, living on the rue de Maubeuge in the 9th *arrondissement* in Paris, until her own early death in July 1939. War was looming and there was little to keep Teddy in France. As a British citizen, he soon moved to London where aunts and uncles were living.

A natural choice

The invasion of Poland by massive German forces on 1st September 1939, in a trumped-up response to a staged 'Polish attack' on a German radio station at Gleiwitz in Upper Silesia, was not entirely a surprise to the British. Neville Chamberlain's claim of 'peace for our time' on 30th September 1938 had seemed increasingly hollow to the British in 1939 and military planning had grown in intensity as the year's events developed. The Cabinet's decision to mobilise for war had come, after a few days of vacillation, on 24th August. Following the British declaration of war against Germany on 3rd September and the rapid defeat of Poland by Germany and the USSR, however, little military action occurred for the next eight months. This was the period known in Britain as the Phoney War and in Germany as *Sitzkrieg* – 'sitting war'.

Teddy Bisset enlisted for military service on Friday, 15th December 1939. The USSR had invaded Finland two weeks earlier, despite the latter's declaration of neutrality, and was meeting tough resistance. But the news that gripped the British public that weekend was the dramatic fate of the German cruiser *Admiral Graf Spee*, damaged in what became known as the Battle of the River Plate. On the Sunday, denied leave to remain in the port of Montevideo by neutral Uruguay, her captain scuttled the warship in the harbour.

Legislation made British men (and women) between the ages of 18 and 41 liable to conscription from September 1939, but the process was in practice graduated according to age and marital status. Single men were called up first. Teddy was 24 years old when he joined the Army in December as a member of the Field Security Police.[2] We will learn later what a misleading term this was for people whose role, according to Captain Sir Basil Bartlett, one of the first Field Security Officers, was to 'thwart enemy attempts at espionage, sabotage and propaganda'.[3] Teddy trained at Mytchett Hutments near Aldershot, with a group of men described by journalist and fellow-trainee Malcolm Muggeridge – whose account of his wartime experience often drips with understated irony – as:

> ranging between carpet-sellers from Baghdad and modern language teachers in grammar schools and colleges ... tourist agency men, unfrocked priests who had lived irregularly in Venice or Rome, and contraceptive salesmen who had roamed the world.[4]

A key criterion for recruitment was competency in foreign languages, so Teddy's selection was no surprise.

The Field Security training course covered a remarkable amount of ground in the two weeks: weapon training with pistols, counter-espionage, interrogation technique, and riding the disparate range of the motorcycles with which the Sections were equipped. Lance-Corporal Bisset, as he was by then, did not get much opportunity for a break over Christmas and New Year. On 15th January he took ship for France with No 20 Field Security Section, landing at Cherbourg, but eventually transferred to 24 Section on its arrival in March to support

---

[2] This was at the time the correct term, but I will use the less confusing Field Security Section or FSS in the rest of this book.

[3] *My First War: An Army Officer's journal for May 1940: through Belgium to Dunkirk*, Sir Basil Bartlett, 1940.

[4] *Chronicles of Wasted Time, vol.2: The Infernal Grove*, Malcolm Muggeridge, 1973, p.86.

50th (Northumbrian) Division as part of the British Expeditionary Force. An intelligence officer in the 50th Division Headquarters was a certain Maurice Buckmaster, who will play an important role in this chapter and later in the book.

Teddy's experience of living in France made him a good choice for the Section's dealings with the local populace. However, he did not stay long with 24 FSS. In late April, he was sent to be secretary to Captain Edwin Whetmore, who was a Liaison Officer to French Intelligence in Lille. Whetmore was later to become Deputy Head of SOE's Security Section.

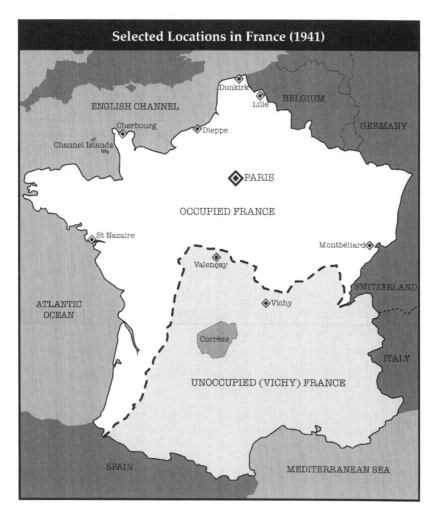

Selected Locations in France (1941)

The stay in Lille was destined to be a short one, as Hitler brought *Sitzkrieg* to an abrupt end. The German invasion of Norway had been launched on 8th April and British troops were supporting the small Norwegian Army in their ultimately unsuccessful defence. On 10th May, however, German forces launched their lightning *Blitzkrieg* attack on Belgium, Luxembourg, the Netherlands and France. In London, Neville Chamberlain resigned and Winston Churchill became Prime Minister. The city of Lille, defended by two French Corps, was besieged in the last days of May before capitulating on 1st June. Defence of the 'Lille Pocket' delayed the German advance by a few days and allowed most of the British force to concentrate at Dunkirk under fierce attack from the Luftwaffe and – famously – escape to southern England with the help of a flotilla of small boats. Whether Captain Whetmore and his new secretary were trapped in Lille during the siege and, if so, how they escaped the fate of the 35,000 French and British troops marched away to captivity is lost to history. How Teddy got home is also unclear, but he and Whetmore may first have followed the French Government as it relocated from Paris to Bordeaux on about 10th June. He did return to England, but not until late June, long after the Dunkirk evacuation was completed and after the final French surrender on 22nd June. He arrived back to find, if not chaos, then turmoil. His links with Field Security had been severed when he left 24 Section, and he returned to find that the Sections had been reorganised following the Allied defeat, while he was still in France. His parent Field Security Wing had moved from Mytchett to Sheerness on the Kent coast, but in view of the potential threat of invasion it had soon relocated to King Alfred's College in Winchester. Teddy reported there for duty.

Higher-level organisational change was under way at the same time. The British Army's Intelligence Corps had been disbanded after the First World War, and what intelligence coverage the British Expeditionary Force had was due to relatively *ad hoc* preparation since 1937, through the initiative of individual staff officers like Colonel Martin and Major Templer. An obvious lesson in mid-1940 was the need for a proper intelligence organisation. The Intelligence

Corps was re-established on 19th July and, along with its other roles, took over responsibility for Field Security from the Corps of Military Police. Its headquarters was at Oriel College, Oxford, and its Depot and Field Security Training Centre at Winchester. On arriving there, Teddy spent a short time at the Depot, but by mid-July he was 'back with my good old friends that I had in France',[5] in a Field Security Section attached to 151st Infantry Brigade at Wraxhall Manor in Dorset, lodging with a motherly Mrs Clarke and travelling around the local area by motorcycle. The Brigade was preparing to defend southern England against the expected German invasion, so the counter-intelligence role of Teddy and his comrades was to investigate suspicious activity – claimed sightings of enemy agents, breaches of security by soldiers among the local people – in the Brigade's area of responsibility. Meanwhile, he was developing an increasingly serious relationship with 'Win'.

Winfred

Winfred Wordsworth Marshall, universally known as 'Win', was a 23-year old budding journalist from Cottesloe, Western Australia, and an accomplished pianist. She had come to London in March 1939, having in 1936 received an award of £50 per year for two years of piano tuition at the Royal College of Music. A Tchaikovsky concerto she played in a concert in Karrakatta, Perth, in December 1938 was effectively her farewell for what her parents expected to be a two-year absence.

Teddy had met Win before he deployed and, by the time he wrote to her from 'somewhere in France' in mid-June 1940, he was 'still alive after some exciting times' and surprisingly, perhaps deliberately, positive. He and Whetmore must have been aware of the severity of the French and British defeat. He had been able to save the French perfume he had promised to buy for her, but he was not sure whether

[5] This and subsequent quotes from Bisset/Marshall letters are from the Marshall archive deposited at the Imperial War Museum, London (IWM 11934).

he would get to England before Win left for Australia. He must have delivered the gift, because she later used the perfume to scent her notepaper in a letter to him.

Pre-war photograph of Win Marshall in magazine

Win's parents in Cottesloe were concerned about their young daughter's safety and kept up an increasing pressure for her to come home. They wrote to her and to Western Australia's representative in London, trying to arrange a sea passage. Win, though, felt an affinity with Britain. She wrote in April 1940 for an Australian magazine about Lady Frances Ryder, who kept open house for soldiers from every part of the Empire and where you might see 'an Australian Air Force boy talking to a Canadian soldier, a South African art student comparing notes with a New Zealand university graduate'. Win was torn between family ties in Australia and her determination not to desert the Londoners, who by September 1940 were under nightly bombardment by the Luftwaffe. She was receiving piano tuition at the Royal College of Music. And of course there was Teddy.

Now Acting Sergeant Bisset, Teddy enjoyed a week's leave in London with Win and other friends and relatives in August 1940. He had a narrow escape on his way back to Dorset when his train was almost hit by a German bomb. In mid-October, he was sent to act as liaison and interpreter for French sailors at Trentham Park near Stoke-on-Trent, an uninspiring duty but even less so after the French had departed; he was put in charge of the stores. His relationship with

Win was his main focus. He had written to her parents in Australia and, two days before Christmas, he received their reply. They thought he might be running after their daughter because of the sudden passion 'that takes everybody during wartime', but he was determined to convince them of his sincerity. Win was dependent on her parents for financial support and became both worried and depressed about her situation. The stress of the bombing cannot have helped. Even though the Midlands were bombed, Win was seeing more of the war in London than was Teddy in Stoke-on-Trent. She worked each night with the Women's Voluntary Service running a mobile canteen. She saw her share of destruction and death.

Into SOE

In January 1941, Teddy returned to the Intelligence Corps Depot at Winchester, to a stricter regime than he had experienced at Trentham. Despite reversion to the rank of lance-corporal, however, military life was very soon to become more interesting. Edwin Whetmore, now a major, had in November 1940 become deputy head of the Special Operations Executive's newly formed Security Section, consisting at first only of Lieutenant-Colonel Calthrop and himself. Whetmore was given the task of recruiting personnel. In December, he obtained War Office authority to 'requisition' three Field Security Sections to support SOE (more widely known under its cover name of 'Inter-Services Research Bureau') from the Director of Military Intelligence. SOE officers interviewed 'volunteers' at Winchester, to assess their ability to judge character and their knowledge of the languages and cultures of enemy-occupied countries. The Sections were duly formed. Teddy Bisset was among the twelve members of one of these, No 64 Section, formed on 1st February 1941 under the command of Lieutenant Thomas Brown and established near Guildford. Teddy shared a 'billet' with Gilbert Smith.

Understandably, Teddy had never been open in his letters to Win about his Army duties. Now, though, he became even more circumspect. As we will learn in more detail later, the primary responsibility of the Field Security Sections in SOE was the security of agents preparing to undertake secret and dangerous missions in enemy-controlled territory. Security had always been at the back of the minds of those setting up SOE, of course. The phrase SOE was itself secret; the anodyne-sounding name Inter-Services Research Bureau explained the range of different uniforms worn by those seen entering and leaving the Baker Street headquarters in London.

SOE was still finding its feet, in security as in everything else, so the Sections' early duties mostly involved the physical security of SOE's various establishments. This was not to be merely guard duty, though. The developing primary role of the Field Security NCOs was to accompany trainees through their various courses to assess their reliability. So, while Teddy did his share of boring duty, keeping the Section office in Guildford manned seven days a week, he looked forward to the next 'job'. He put no more than this in writing, but it involved travelling to the various SOE training establishments throughout England and Scotland, living and working alongside trainee agents and compiling weekly reports on them. While this was often seen by the trainers as tantamount to Gestapo tactics, the Field Security personnel would do everything they could to instil a sense of security in the agents. Their survival – and that of others with whom they would be in contact – was at stake. The role with SOE also included some of the more conventional Field Security activity: visiting pubs close to training establishments to find out if word of their activities had got out, liaising with local police, testing perimeter security, assessing how well documents were safeguarded.

Teddy Bisset was a popular and reliable colleague, by now a sergeant (again!) with a great deal of counter-espionage experience, so he was able to get alongside agents, befriend them in a genuine way and help them to improve their chances of survival in their dangerous future missions. His qualities were recognised, and in late May 1941 he was able to write to Win's parents in Western Australia to tell them he was to be commissioned in mid-June as a lieutenant. He did not tell them that he would be joining SOE's French Section, which recruited agents and planned their missions, both in German-occupied northern France and in the southern part of France governed by the 'independent' Vichy regime. His Field Security Officer, Thomas Brown, was delighted by Bisset's promotion, not knowing that this was but the first of seven of the Section of twelve who would be commissioned.

Teddy's postal address was now a suitably anonymous 'Box 900, Western District, London W1', but his place of work in London was in the French Section Headquarters at Norgeby House off Baker Street or – to meet agents, who were not allowed into the HQ for security reasons – in an apartment in Orchard Court on Portman Square. He was still travelling widely within Britain, frustrated with the time Win's letters took to get to him.

Win had by March 1941 been resident in Britain for two years, understood that she would be subject to conscription and volunteered for the Civil Nursing Reserve. After training for a month, she moved in late May 1941 to the Three Counties Emergency Hospital in Bedfordshire, 45 miles north of London. She was convinced that she would not be able to return to Australia before the end of the war, as all ships were being requisitioned as soon as they were built. Teddy felt that she was in any case safer in England than on the high seas. So she stayed in England, and Teddy met her on the platform of Finsbury Park station for their short times together.

The King's Commission

Meanwhile, Teddy was finding his way as a newly commissioned General List officer and a relatively junior member of the French, or 'F', Section staff. Soon, and certainly by January 1942, he was working as a conducting officer, accompanying agents through every stage of their training courses at the SOE's various training schools and reporting on their progress and suitability for the role. As individuals arriving in London who were 'pure' French were expected to join Charles de Gaulle's Free French, many F Section agents were of British, Anglo-French or Canadian extraction. After a potential agent had been interviewed, screened for medical or security issues and given a clean bill of health in both senses, the training followed a broadly similar pattern for all. It started at Wanborough.

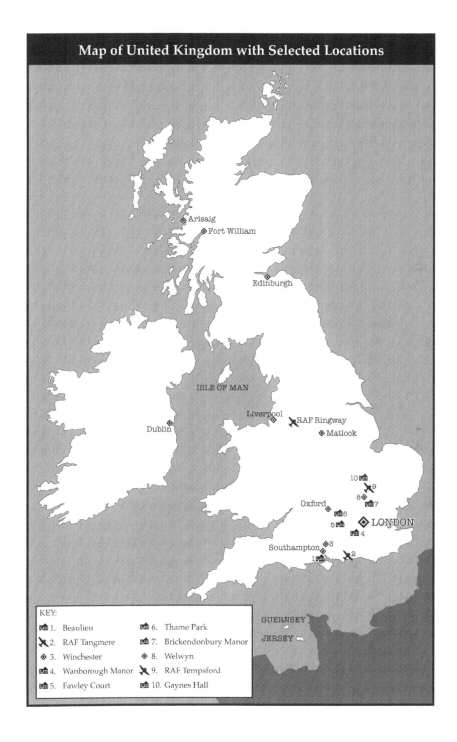

Map of United Kingdom with Selected Locations

Arisaig
Fort William

Edinburgh

ISLE OF MAN

Liverpool
RAF Ringway
Matlock

Dublin

10
9
8
Oxford 7
6
5 LONDON
4
Southampton 3
1 2

KEY:

1. Beaulieu
2. RAF Tangmere
3. Winchester
4. Wanborough Manor
5. Fawley Court
6. Thame Park
7. Brickendonbury Manor
8. Welwyn
9. RAF Tempsford
10. Gaynes Hall

GUERNSEY
JERSEY

Wanborough Manor was an Elizabethan country house near Guildford in Surrey, one of many requisitioned by the SOE. In the grounds and the surrounding countryside, groups of a dozen or so trainee agents were given physical fitness training and instructed in navigation, weapon handling, basic demolition and living off the land. But the primary aim was to weed out those who were unsuitable, so the group were monitored by the conducting officers and Field Security personnel twenty-four hours a day. Up to this point, they had been given only the vaguest indication of the role of SOE. They slept in a dormitory, with Teddy occupying the end bed near the entrance. One of the party, a Londoner who had been a tailor, caused some consternation by talking loudly in his sleep – in English, which could be dangerous if he was posing as a Frenchman – but after urgent discussion among the staff was permitted to stay.

After Wanborough, the half-dozen who were allowed to continue with the training moved for several weeks to northern Scotland, where much of Inverness-shire had been designated one of several military 'Protected Areas'. The headquarters were at Arisaig House, and French Section used this property and others nearby, such as Meoble Lodge, next to Loch Morar. In the rugged Highland landscape, the trainees were brought to a high standard of physical fitness and paramilitary skill, starting each day with a 5-mile run and continuing with weapons training, demolition and unarmed combat. They were taught by a Highland ghillie how to stalk a stag; if they could master this, they would have no difficulty creeping up on a sentry.

At a time when rationing in Britain meant everyone was hungry all the time, they were fed royally – steak, eggs, kippers for breakfast – to build up their strength. Even so, they poached salmon, exploding a detonator in a sand-filled tin to stun the fish, and tried to get it back undetected by gamekeepers and staff. Teddy wrote to Win that he was being well fed, but reported on the bitter cold in the large rambling house in which they were accommodated. When the students were sent out on night marches to plant dummy charges on the steam railway line, the drivers knew to look out for them and pelted the intruders with large lumps of coal if they spotted them. As a punishment for being seen, Teddy made them collect all of the pieces of coal and carry them back for the fires in the Mess accommodation. More authentic demolition training, with live explosives, used redundant rail track and rolling stock. Parachute training took place at the parachute training school at Ringway – today's Manchester Airport – where the SOE students lived in houses separate from other parachute trainees.

After a few days' leave following the paramilitary training, the students moved on – again with Teddy as conducting officer – to 'Finishing School'. This took place in the complex of requisitioned buildings at Beaulieu, the ancestral estate of the Montagu family in the New Forest, where the sequestrated new occupants were known locally as the 'Hush-Hush Troops'. Different nationalities were separated from each other; one property used for F Section students was Boarmans, an isolated building approached along a long track over a cattle grid. The first women agents were also trained here.

The students, speaking French with the instructors and each other, here learned how to become successful undercover agents in France. Still monitored by Teddy and by Field Security NCOs, they were taught to organise an undercover Resistance group, to arrange clandestine communications, to position dead letter boxes, to establish safe houses and danger signals, to recognise the different enemy security agencies, to concoct and maintain cover stories, to avoid arousing suspicion at checkpoints, to pick locks, to break into locked buildings, to disseminate propaganda and – importantly – to resist interrogation.

The students practised these new skills in exercises, perhaps making a secret contact and evading detection by watchers in a local town like Bournemouth. The main emphasis was on security, and Teddy's counter-intelligence experience was of benefit to his 'brood'. He was able to encourage them to take the security exercises seriously, even if they recognised the 'German soldier' who rousted them out of bed in the middle of the night as the Mess barman in real life. It might help them to survive. Some, to their eventual cost, took little notice.

After Finishing School and any specialist courses individuals needed – such as sabotage or operating clandestine radios – Teddy's agents might have to wait for several weeks or even months until the weather, the moon phase and the tactical situation were right for their night insertion into France. But this tense time was not spent idly waiting in the 'Holding School' for the starting gun. The agents were briefed about the area into which they would be inserted, the local Resistance groups and the objectives of the mission. They concocted their cover stories and were tested on every detail. They were offered a cyanide capsule as a potential escape from torture. They wrote letters to family and a will. And Teddy stayed with them until they flew from the RAF airfield at Tempsford in Bedfordshire to be parachuted or from RAF Tangmere in Sussex for a night landing by Lysander aircraft in France.

On operations

Teddy's role was not as passive as it might sound. On 1st June 1942, he told Win that he would have to go away on a course lasting two to fifteen days, depending on the weather. This was probably a course at the Ringway parachute training school. He was back in London by the next weekend, but on Sunday 7th told Win that he would soon be going away on a 'rather special job' but that it would not be dangerous. He was interviewed for this the following day and subsequently underwent training with Captain Percy 'Peter' Harratt and another officer for what would be called *Operation Knotgrass/Traveller*, the special operations element of *Operation Rutter*, the raid on Dieppe planned for early July. Teddy impressed the training school with his general attitude and his great efficiency. Jacques Vaillant de Guélis reported to French Section that Bisset was training a party of Canadians (perhaps French-speaking *Québécois*) 'with no previous knowledge of street-fighting, the Sten gun or grenades'; he was doing it well, wrote de Guélis, and had the Canadians' complete confidence.[6]

---

[6] TNA HS 9/158/2.

Operation Rutter was the first attempt by the Allies to try a major amphibious landing on the French coast and hold territory for a limited period. Bad weather and fears of German awareness of the potential attack led to last-minute cancellation. Ten weeks later, a scaled-down version of the operation became *Operation Jubilee*.

In the meantime, Teddy was gaining experience on another operation. He warned Win on Thursday 23rd July 1942 that he would be leaving London that night for a while. He travelled by sleeper train to the Southwest and wrote to her on Saturday 24th that he was 'somewhere in England by the sea', 'living the life of a rich man' with a 'good billet, bathing and swimming' and enjoying 'rowing in the morning and sailing in the afternoon'. On Monday, he 'went fishing in a trawler' in rough seas, returning at 2.30 a.m. after twelve hours in the 'cursed ship'. He was 'sailing' again on Wednesday and Thursday and starting to enjoy it. He next wrote ten days later, reporting that he was 'just back from a job' and 'very tired [even] after a long night in bed' but 'happy with life'.

His reports to HQ on *Operation Guillotine*, for that was its name, were both more formal and more candid. He and his comrades left the Isles of Scilly at 16.00 hrs on Sunday 2nd August in a boat known officially as P11. This was an inshore fishing vessel of the *pinasse* type, the *Ar-Mouscoul*, that had been found part-submerged in the fishing port of Newlyn in Cornwall. Raised, repaired and fitted with a new diesel engine, she was capable of 9 knots.

Teddy and his comrades were tasked with transferring a shipment to a French fishing boat: explosives, incendiaries, Colt pistols and ammunition, disguised in a French fish box, French paint drums and a French lifebelt respectively. The trawler picked up a fighter escort and sailed to the planned rendezvous with *L'Audacieux,* from the fishing port of Léchiagat near the île d'Yeu, south of the German naval base at Saint-Nazaire. They eventually spotted the French vessel some 15 to 20 miles away from the agreed spot; 'That's not so far', shrugged the Breton skipper. The French did not provide the recognition signal or passwords, but eventually came alongside and three crew members came aboard the SOE 'trawler' for coffee.

Uncertain what kind of vessel he was expecting, the French skipper had been wary of providing the signal. The French were unwilling to take the whole consignment, in case of German spot checks, and a further problem arose. Three other crew members, left on board the French vessel, had been unaware of the planned rendezvous, but now were, and one of them was a drinker who talked freely when drunk. Bisset considered bringing that man back to England as a prisoner, but decided that the French crew would have too much explaining to do on their return. He had no alternative but to tell these other three men what was going on.

In his report, Bisset made his concerns about this unsatisfactory dilemma very clear, as well as passing on the views of the Bretons regarding the inadequate camouflage of the containers. He suggested that the problems of rendezvous could be avoided by leaving the explosives in submerged waterproof containers for the recipients to pick up later. Also, the British boat was not particularly well camouflaged; it did not carry sails and lacked proper fishing gear, so did not fit in well with the French boats.

Yet another issue surfaced. On their way back to the Isles of Scilly on the night of Wednesday 5th August, the team had spotted an apparently damaged U-boat being escorted by three German surface vessels. They had tried to radio the position to set up an air attack, but were unable to make contact. Not only had the opportunity to attack the four German vessels been lost through the lack of radio contact, said Bisset, but the confidence of the crew in calling for any support if discovered had also been severely shaken.

Not surprisingly, Teddy was not aware of the full picture. The operation had originally been set up in cooperation with SIS and the Free French in London, to bring a French Communist representative back to England for discussions about future weapon deliveries. Also, the French had stated only two days before the operation that arms must be packed in the boxes used by prawn fishermen and were meant to be bringing a sample of these boxes to the rendezvous. None of this occurred. The operation in which Teddy and his comrades risked their lives had fallen victim to bureaucratic communication failures and was at best a partial success. These were still early days for covert insertion into occupied France and lessons were being learned. The main conclusion was that air-dropping supplies would be a more secure method in future. But competition for aircraft sorties was intense.

Very soon afterwards, Teddy, together with his F Section colleague Jacques Vaillant de Guélis in a party led by Peter Harratt, was involved in the unsuccessful Allied raid on Dieppe. This was *Operation Jubilee*, the successor to *Rutter*. Launched on 19th August 1942, it was the first major raid on the French coast and involved 6,000 mostly Canadian troops, of whom two-thirds were captured, injured or killed. The operation, aiming to hold a major French port for a significant period, failed on most counts and shaped Allied planning for the timing and scale of *Operation Overlord*, the D-Day invasion. The reasons for launching the disastrous raid are controversial to this day.

Teddy Bisset (far right) as a Canadian Captain in 1942 before the Dieppe Raid, with comrades, including Peter Harratt (next to Bisset, wearing beret).

On Sunday 16th August, three days before the raid, Teddy had written to Win saying that he would be going away the next day. He did not know how long he would be away, but, he again said, 'Don't be worried, it won't be a very dangerous job'. He wore uniform appropriate to the role he was trying to portray, and Win kept a photograph after the war 'from the Dieppe Raid' of Teddy wearing the battledress of a Captain in the Canadian Army.

The team were to establish a headquarters near Dieppe's Dental School, with anti-aircraft protection from a sergeant and six soldiers of 16th Battery, 3rd Canadian Light Anti-Aircraft Regiment. A total of eight or nine members of SOE participated in the raid. Harratt's orders were to search the Town Hall and carry out a special mission. Little information is available on their 'special mission', whether it was providing cash for local Resistance fighters, helping to capture an urgently needed four-rotor Enigma coding machine or simply collecting unspecified secret German documents. More generally, SOE was very keen to obtain samples of everyday items. While all units involved in the raid were briefed to collect enemy weapons and military equipment, SOE wanted material like toothbrushes, foodstuffs, civilian gas masks and underwear. Facsimiles of such items could then be crafted and used to equip agents. Also, the mysterious 'Canadian' Field Security sergeant who accompanied RAF technical expert Jack Nissenthall during the Dieppe raid, on his mission to recover information and equipment from a Freya radar station, may have been from SOE. The sergeant was tasked to ensure that Nissenthall did not fall into enemy hands alive. I have found no proof that Sergeant Frank Donaldson of 65 Field Security Section was this man, but his personal file shows that he was a member of the Dieppe party.

Captain Harratt's team spent five hours in a landing craft within hailing distance of the beach, waiting to disembark, but were eventually ordered to withdraw, and their mission was therefore not accomplished. Teddy was fortunate not to be killed or captured during the tragic operation. Peter Harratt was wounded in the knee by shrapnel while holding offshore. Major David Wyatt, the officer at Lord Louis Mountbatten's Combined Operations HQ responsible for liaison with Baker Street, did not return from the Dieppe raid. He was stranded ashore and killed while attempting to contact local

Resistance groups. The liaison between the two HQs, one-way as it may have been, dried up completely for several months.

On 20th August, the day after the Dieppe Raid, Teddy was back in London. He arrived at Finsbury Park station an hour late and just missed Win, having collected his pay – they were paid in cash, in crisp new £5 notes – and having had a good welcome at F Section. One can imagine their relief at seeing him, as the classified intelligence came in about the disaster at Dieppe. He told Win nonchalantly that he had arranged a few days 'near Guildford', his 'code' for Wanborough Manor.

At the end of September in the same year, Teddy was admitted to the Royal Masonic Hospital in Hammersmith, West London, for surgery: what he called 'a small cut'. He stayed there a little over a week while he and Win were simultaneously making wedding preparations. On 31st October 1942, having received a telegram from Australia giving her parents' permission, Win and Teddy were married at St Martin-in-the-Fields Church, just off Trafalgar Square in the centre of London. Peter Harratt, leader of the SOE team at Dieppe, and Jacques de Guélis were ushers at the wedding.

Captain Bisset soon started training for a new 'special' raiding party, this time involving dropping by parachute to sabotage electricity pylons, for which his small team trained at Special Training School 17, Brickendonbury Manor. The training culminated with a period at a 'Holding School' in December 1942 at STS 44, probably located at Gorse Hill near Godalming in southern England. The Commandant of the school accompanied them to parachute training at Ringway. Five members of this *Operation Hangman* party were removed during training, three of them for medical or psychological reasons. One member was observed never to be 'one of the party'; he made it clear that 'he could not accept to be led by less competent men than himself'.[7] Despite his lack of teamwork, this man was clearly considered very competent, because he was withdrawn and prepared for a lone sabotage mission under civilian cover.

---

[7] The National Archives (TNA) HS 6/354.

Teddy's view, as team leader, of his rather dysfunctional group was that teams should not consist exclusively of officers. In his view, only the leader and deputy should be commissioned officers, the remainder being NCOs and soldiers. Well-trained soldiers would obey orders without complaint or argument and always appreciate good treatment. In contrast, some of the *Hangman* team forgot that they had to take orders, not least because of the 'fuss' made of them during training. Holding his team together during the escape phase, once the two-hour sabotage attack was completed, was of particular concern to Teddy. The plan for escape seemed rather vague. Collaboration with MI9, one of the agencies tasked with setting up escape lines for downed Allied airmen, appears not to have been feasible at this stage of the war. Teddy did not relish the thought of being 'trapped' in rural France awaiting the Allied invasion, with little opportunity to contribute further to the war effort.

Nevertheless, Captain Bisset 'looked after his party well and set a good example'. On New Year's Eve, with the reduced team waiting for the go-ahead, he made his own report on the proposed mission. He reported the difficulty of keeping the skills of young, inexperienced men honed during a prolonged waiting period. Also, in view of the danger of being treated as a spy and summarily shot, he was very keen to do the operation in uniform rather than civilian clothes, and had convinced his comrades that this would be preferable. He put the arguments against civilian disguise on raiding parties to his superiors, and suggested that the party be equipped for escape with RAF aircrew survival dinghies, which they could carry for the 24 miles from the targets to the coast and then use for a 95-mile sea journey to Spain. Although he was showing bold original thinking, with hindsight his optimism for this method of escape seems excessive. Also, with an eye to the psychology of such teams, he pleaded for rather less morbid code names than *Guillotine* and *Hangman*; 'the jobs in themselves smell of death quite enough'.

One aspect of the preparation for *Operation Hangman* is intriguing. While training for the operation, Teddy claimed that he had made fifteen jumps, whereas the Ringway parachute school's records showed only four, a figure he quietly accepted after further consideration. This is a large discrepancy and cannot be laid at the door of his own pride or dishonesty. The school may not have accounted for jumps he had made with trainees.

As it turned out, the *Hangman* raid appears not to have gone ahead, perhaps because the team was too depleted. Captain Bisset was himself withdrawn from training for *Operation Hangman* in January 1943 for medical reasons. He had suffered for some time from a chronic skin complaint, but this is unlikely to have been enough to disqualify him for the planned operation. The problem may have been a foot injury he had sustained in 1942, from which he eventually recovered fully.

Uncertainty

A period of difficult uncertainty for Teddy followed. He seems to have stayed at STS 44 for a while, at the Commandant's request, and for a few days Win 'coincidentally' rented a cottage near Dorking, not far from where he was working. However, he was then abruptly recalled to French Section, to report with his kit on Monday 12th April 1943 and work for a while as a French Section staff officer. He helped to plan operations, saw agents off to their hazardous assignments, arranged messages to be transmitted by the BBC and gave their family members the meagre information that could be released to them. 'Your brother has recently contacted us; he has arrived safely at his destination and is well.' 'We continue to have excellent news of your daughter, who is very well indeed and sends much love to you.'

During this period, Teddy and his French Section colleague Flight Officer Vera Atkins carried on a lengthy, morale-boosting correspondence with the mother of Pearl Witherington. This courageous agent had been sent to France as a courier for Maurice Southgate and ended up leading a Resistance network, or 'circuit', of her own after his arrest. Her mother had been told she had gone to North Africa. Pearl had set up arrangements for the Section to send her mother a monthly allowance to be deducted from her pay, with extra gifts for family birthdays and Christmas. On occasion, Teddy was able to suggest that he could forward a personal letter to Pearl, written on thin paper.[8]

Alongside the family welfare aspects, more serious matters occasionally arose. A gossipy letter intercepted by censors in West Africa, a few weeks before she was due to be deployed, suggested that Pearl might be back in France. This was potentially dangerous for her, but investigation unravelled the details and revealed that the risk was small; she was allowed to go.[9]

Although fulfilling a staff role, Teddy was still being considered for operations. He completed a three-week course in industrial sabotage at Special Training School 17, Brickendonbury Manor in Hertfordshire, from 26th April to 15th May 1943. This was presumably in preparation for a further raid in France, but by June he was applying for a transfer out of SOE, desiring 'a more regimental type of employment'. Win was by now pregnant, so he may have wanted more stability, but no wartime service was going to give him more time at home or, probably, any less danger. Indeed, the turning point of the war was approaching, when irregular warfare and encouraging resistance to occupation may have seemed to be giving way to larger-scale campaigns, in which he was keen to participate. The Allied invasion of France was widely expected to be launched in the second half of 1943.

French Section recommended Teddy for either the Intelligence Corps or Combined Operations, but the interviews did not go well. He was accepted for neither. From September, he served as a Briefing Officer in French Section, briefing agents in organising Resistance groups, 'life in the field', French topography and reception arrangements for supply drops and flights. With his extensive experience, this was a role he could fulfil with distinction as he travelled to SOE training schools in Scotland and closer to home. Some of the briefing was at STS 61, the French Section 'Holding

---

[8] TNA HS 9/355/2.
[9] TNA 9/355/2 D/CE to A/CD, 14th September 1943.

School' at Gaynes Hall near St Neots in Cambridgeshire. Win eventually tired of the delay in getting letters to Teddy via the secure but laborious PO Box in London and sent them direct to the country house.

Even before the USA entered the war following the Pearl Harbor attack in December 1941, the war was a global one. Soldiers, sailors and airmen from every part of the British Empire were part of the Allied effort. Win's brother Lloyd, who had trained as a navigator in the Royal Australian Air Force, arrived in England in mid-April 1943 to join the fight against the Axis Powers. After a spell at RAF Pocklington near York, he moved closer to his sister, serving at RAF Graveley near Huntingdon as a Pathfinder navigator in Lancaster bombers. He would be awarded the Distinguished Flying Cross in February 1945.

Win and Teddy had at first lived in an apartment just off Hammersmith Road in West London, but the owner wished to move back in, so they took a room in a boarding house not far away, at 18 Melbury Road, near Holland Park. No 18's claim to fame was that the artist William Holman Hunt had been one of its previous owners and had painted one version of 'The Light of the World' in his studio there. More obscurely, they may not have been aware that down the road at No 1 was a house that had been the headquarters until 1926 of SOE's 'rival' organisation SIS. On 23rd November 1943, as Allied troops were slowly advancing through mainland Italy, Win gave birth to a daughter, Laura.

One aspect of large-scale training that was increasingly urgent, and with which Captain Bisset as French Section Briefing Officer may have been involved, was the preparation of Jedburgh teams. In order to disrupt German opposition to the planned Allied invasion of mainland Europe, SOE and its clandestine American equivalent, the Office of Strategic Services (OSS), cooperated in training 300 men to drop into occupied territory, in teams of three. A Jedburgh team in France generally consisted of an officer from SOE or OSS, an officer from the Free French forces and a non-commissioned radio operator. The teams had the mission of equipping, organising and training local

Resistance fighters to sabotage lines of communication and immobilise German reinforcements. With the Allied invasion imminent, concerns about encouraging large-scale uprising, and the reprisals they would trigger, had become much less of an issue. After toughening up in commando training in Scotland, the teams underwent the main Jedburgh training together at Milton Hall near Peterborough, learning small group tactics and sabotage techniques, while conversing with each other in the language of the country they were about to 'visit'. D-Day was approaching.

Mission Tilleul

In early 1944, the tide of war was inexorably turning against the Axis Powers. Royal Air Force and US Army Air Force bombing was devastating Germany. German forces were retreating from the Red Army's advance in the east. Mass American troop formations were arriving in Britain in preparation for opening the Second Front in the West. Teddy, Win and baby Laura were still living together in London, unlike many soldiers and their families who were separated for years at a time. Even so, Teddy was frequently absent, and Win's mother Gladys had braved the six-week sea journey from Western Australia to support her daughter and new granddaughter.

On 2nd June 1944, four days before D-Day, Captain Bisset formally applied to be released from his F Section staff duties 'to take up other employment in the field which has been offered to me'. He was transferred to the 'F Agents List' on the same day. Stringent security constraints restricted movements into the field of personnel who might be captured in possession of highly classified information. French Section had to make assurances that Captain Bisset had not had access to any SIS documents or correspondence during his months as Briefing Officer, nor to any security information since being earmarked for a mission.

Teddy started to prepare for '*Mission Tilleul*', frustrated by the constant changes of plan in 'the office' about the mission. While he was training and preparing, Win and baby Laura had moved with Win's mother to Leverington Hall in Cambridgeshire, escaping the increasing threat to London of V1 'flying bombs' and V2 rockets. They stayed with friends, who were 'charming and kind, English country folk at their best'. The night before his departure for the mission, Teddy and Win went for dinner at Oddenino's restaurant near Piccadilly Circus, and he made his farewells.

Teddy and Win before *Mission Tilleul*, 1944

The team of seven men took off on the night of 7th/8th July 1944 from RAF Harrington, Northamptonshire, in US Army Air Force *Operation Carpetbagger* B24 Liberator aircraft, and parachuted into the hilly Haute-Vienne region of southwest France. Each man had 44 pounds of personal kit, except de Guélis, who had 186 pounds. With them in the three-aircraft formation were twenty-one containers of arms, explosives, radios with trickle chargers and petrol generators, food and medical supplies.

They were received by Philippe Liewer (field name *Hamlet*) of SOE's *Salesman* circuit at a drop zone near Sussac, 40 kilometres southeast of Limoges. The remoteness of the area was of the kind that inspired an SOE veteran to say that 'France was made by God with SOE in mind'.[10]

---

[10] IWM Oral History 18594 'SOE in France'.

The team had been given false French papers and civilian clothes for emergency use, but this was always understood to be a uniformed mission. However, this was not a Jedburgh team but an 'inter-allied' mission, jointly led by the impressively tall Major Vaillant de Guélis of F Section and pipe-smoking Commandant Thomas of the FFI (*Forces Françaises de l'Intérieur*).

The team came under direct command of de Gaulle's newly formed Free French HQ, the EMFFI (*État-Major des Forces Françaises de l'Intérieur*), but was to be looked after by F Section officers, with whose methods the majority of the party were familiar and who were at that time being absorbed by the EMFFI. Although the intense political tensions at the higher level are well-documented, relationships between F Section and the Gaullist 'Fighting French' at working level could be good.

The main plan was to organise the *maquis* in sabotage of railway lines and depots, munitions and aircraft factories, electricity supply lines and specific electrical transformers. They were specifically instructed not to destroy dams, power stations and major transformers, but rather to attempt to protect them from destruction by retreating German forces.

The group was not working with a blank canvas. Thanks to circuits like Liewer's *Salesman* and the *Author* circuit – built up by Harry Peulevé and Jacques Poirier and based at Brive-la-Gaillarde – the *maquis* had been developed from a motley assortment of young men, who had disappeared into the hills to avoid compulsory conscription to labour camps in Germany, into a substantial guerrilla force. But they had very few weapons. Supporting the Allied invasion called for more intensive, coordinated and unified operations, supplied with increased amounts of arms and equipment by parachute. Crucially, the *Tilleul* team had to encourage the Gaullist and Communist Resistance groups to set aside their differences and together obstruct German reinforcements rushing to oppose the Allied invasion.

Alongside de Guélis, Thomas and Bisset were Major Ian Mackenzie, medical officer, two wireless (radio) operators, *Matelot* Georges Lannou and Sergeant James Edgar (Intelligence Corps), and

Flight Lieutenant André Simon, responsible for identifying drop zones and organising reception parties. Edgar, who had been a member of No 63 Field Security Section, accompanied the reception parties led by Simon. The latter was a friendly, optimistic man with long experience of SOE operations in France, the son of a renowned wine merchant. Teddy Bisset was given the field name *Adjacent* for the operation, perhaps because his original personal code name, *Drastique*, was too close to André Simon's: *Diastique*.

At Sussac, the team met with Liewer and the Resistance leaders of the Haute-Vienne, quickly realising that the Resistance in the Massif Central was stronger and better organised than they had been led to suppose in England. In the next few days, Liewer introduced them to Resistance leaders in the Corrèze, the isolated area in which they were to operate.

The two main elements in the Corrèze of what were now theoretically unified as the FFI were the Communist-sponsored FTP (*Francs-Tireurs et Partisans*) and the AS (*Armée secrète*). The divisions and mutual animosity between the two were clear, but they were more unified when actually fighting the German occupiers. Altogether, the Resistance groups had about 4,000 properly armed men but a further 15,000 or so awaiting arms. The *Tilleul* group, relying on promises made to them in London, in turn promised substantial deliveries of arms soon. But arms did not start arriving until the first days of August.

The group at first set up headquarters in a house belonging to Justin and Micheline Sauviat in the hamlet of Chadebec, near Bonnefond, although they subsequently moved from place to place for security reasons. The remote wooded area, dotted with small villages and hamlets, was ideal country for the *maquisards* and the Allied troops who were supplying and supporting them. On 13th July, the team inspected the Marèges Dam, which they had received orders to protect, and arranged for the Resistance to mount an enhanced guard on it, but later visits to other dams showed them to be under construction and not to warrant demolition by the Germans. On the same day, Ian Mackenzie reported to London on the local medical situation: 'no surgeon within 30 miles except self, request further medical supplies'.[11] He set up a temporary hospital at Saint-Yrieix-le-Déjalat, operating in an improvised theatre and, according to French colleagues, carrying out some remarkable operations.

Tilleul Group (Bisset third from left)

The team were frustrated by the lack of response by London to a dozen or more radio messages in their first two weeks. Teddy's role was to be the mission's weapons expert, so he was sent off to instruct Resistance fighters in the use of the arms and explosives the team had brought, and to give them some new ideas on the laying of ambushes. He took part in several ambushes himself with the fighters he had trained. As always in his letters, Teddy put a positive spin on his experiences. He somehow got a letter to Win, saying 'we have had a marvellous welcome here and never expected such pleasant work and life. The whole party is pleased and keeping well together so that we make quite a decent company'.

---

[11] TNA HS 6/367.

No plan survives first contact with the enemy, as Helmuth von Moltke more or less said, but relations with Allies can spread just as much 'fog of war'. The plethora of separate and often rival agencies and nationalities in London, prosecuting irregular warfare in different ways, was paralleled by confusion and disagreement about command and control in the field. When a party of about thirty French SAS soldiers and a three-man Jedburgh team arrived in the Corrèze, for example, they did not see themselves as under the direction of the more established *Mission Tilleul*, despite earlier Allied agreements. The demolitions that the two groups were expecting to carry out were no longer necessary – indeed counter-productive – so the Jedburgh team were put in touch with local Resistance groups, while the SAS group operated independently on very successful ambushes and road-mining. They also fought with distinction alongside *maquisards* in the attack on the German garrison at Égletons and subsequent siege of the German redoubt in the town's school. Surprisingly, given the demands on air power at the battle front in northern France, German aircraft attacked the besiegers. Many of the young *maquisards* had not experienced air attack before and were severely shaken. Teddy Bisset went from group to group reassuring them about the limited capabilities of the aircraft and encouraging disciplined anti-aircraft fire by Bren guns when they dived.

Some garrisons had already surrendered, but the *maquis* lifted the siege at Égletons on 18th August and withdrew, when a strong German column was reported to be approaching from Clermont-Ferrand to relieve the Corrèze garrisons. The column camped overnight within yards of Mackenzie's temporary hospital, but the condition of the wounded was too grave for them to be moved, so he and his staff continued their work as if everything were normal. On the column's arrival in Égletons, the Germans destroyed any undamaged houses, but were then themselves bombed by RAF Mosquitoes. After being dissuaded by the *maquis* from carrying out reprisals in Tulle, scene of a previous massacre shortly after D-Day, the column's commander received a recall message. The tide was turning. The column returned the way it had come, under heavy harassment and ambushes. The Germans were in full retreat from France. Paris had been liberated on 25th August and a second Allied force was advancing from Provence in the south. No further German advances into Corrèze took place, and by 22nd August the only Germans there were prisoners, thanks in no small part to the patient coordination of the Resistance groups by the *Tilleul* team.

James Edgar and Teddy Bisset receiving Croix de Guerre

Teddy was able to write to Win on 27th August that 'it is almost all clear as regards the Germans' and found time to start writing a long note to her, although he did not know when he might be able to send it. He was living in an old castle in a small village, eating too well at a small restaurant nearby, being given bouquets and plied with wine, and he had just been kissed by three nice French girls, but he still could not tell her where he was. He still had some work to do, he wrote, but he and his comrades were winding down.

On 17th September, Teddy paraded with about twenty British and American comrades in Limoges to receive the Croix de Guerre with Bronze Star. The war had passed on from Corrèze, but Teddy wrote with concern on 19th September when he heard from an officer who had just left London about V2 rocket attacks on the capital.

Four days later, on Saturday, Teddy and an American colleague and good friend, Captain Ted Fraser, left Limoges in a US Army jeep, to travel via Vichy to Paris and report to the new forward Headquarters there. The war in France apparently behind them, they spent that night at the *Hôtel des Ambassadeurs* in Vichy. Next day, they loaded the jeep with seven cans of petrol, their rucksacks, weapons and personal kit. Teddy, standing on the rear of the jeep, asked a bell-boy to pass him one of the rucksacks from the front. As he was doing so, a shot rang out and Teddy fell to the floor of the jeep. A stretcher was brought to carry him to the nearby hospital, but he died three minutes after being placed on the stretcher.

A Marlin submachine gun had fallen on to the street, the impact had caused the safety lever to shift and a bullet to move into firing position. The bullet had pierced Teddy's heart. On 25th September, Major Ian Mackenzie arrived in Vichy and took charge of the arrangements for Teddy's funeral, which took place that day, three weeks before his 29th birthday, in a Protestant church in the town with a guard of honour from the FFI.

Teddy Bisset's funeral procession, Vichy
(Ian Mackenzie centre right, wearing beret)

Teddy's SOE colleagues rallied round to support Win in her grief. As there was nothing to keep her in England and the widow's pension would be inadequate, she decided to make a fresh start in Australia. With the help of a letter from Colonel Maurice Buckmaster, head of F Section, to Australia House, Win and baby Laura obtained a priority sea passage.

Laura grew up to be a journalist and in 1967 was back in London, where she was married in St Martin-in-the-Fields, the church where her parents' wedding had taken place. Maurice Buckmaster, in the absence of her father, 'gave her away' and the wedding reception was held at the Special Forces Club. Sadly, Laura died in 1974 while working as a journalist in Canberra. Win survived her and lived in Western Australia until 2013, although, writing to Buckmaster from the ship in November 1944 *en route* to Fremantle, she had expressed a wish to return and live in France one day. She remained a resilient woman, staying in touch with Teddy's SOE comrades, including Vera Atkins, the F Section Intelligence Officer who spent months after the war searching for traces of SOE agents in concentration camps. Win wrote for Australian magazines, for example humorously recounting the experience of queueing for food in London under rationing, or recording the return in 1945 of Australian nurses from Japanese captivity.

SOE Memorial at Valençay

The citation for Teddy's posthumous Mention in Despatches describes his engagement in ambushes and organising anti-aircraft fire when under attack, and says 'He showed the highest courage and devotion to duty the whole time he was in the field'. Nevertheless, his name is absent from the memorial at Valençay, dedicated in 1991 to members of F Section who lost their lives in the efforts to liberate France. It is unclear whether this is because his mission was inter-allied and not a 'pure' F Section one or because he was killed accidentally after the liberation, but some see it as an injustice.

Teddy Bisset's personal story illustrates in microcosm many of the themes that will occur in the rest of this book. The disparate political allegiances of those with whom he worked demonstrate SOE's willingness to work with anyone as long as they were anti-Nazi. In France this meant the spectrum from Gaullists to Communists and everything in between. Paradoxically, despite the highly political nature of its activity, SOE was in this sense apolitical. Similarly, Teddy's various activities in Britain and in France, and the people he worked with, together reflect the dual roles of SOE: on the one hand raiding and sabotage, on the other the raising of an army of resisters that would help to overthrow the occupiers when called upon by the invading Allies.

SOE did not just send in undercover 'civilian' agents. It also carried out uniformed short-duration raids – *coups de main* – and similar missions. In doing so, it cooperated with, but was often seen as treading on the toes of, other agencies like Combined Operations or the Free French forces. The rivalry was fuel to the fire of SOE's negative reputation with more conventional forces and with SIS. Also, although Teddy was officially given the status of F Section 'agent' in June 1944, he was not an SOE secret agent as the term is popularly understood. Indeed, he was uncomfortable with operating undercover in civilian clothes, much preferring to be in uniform. Finally, he is a good example of the Field Security personnel who were not just 'guarding agents', but did much more besides. We will meet more of them in the coming chapters.

CHAPTER 2

The Intelligence Connection

'A new organisation is being established to co-ordinate all action,
by way of subversion and sabotage, against the enemy overseas ...
known as the Special Operations Executive'
Neville Chamberlain, Lord President of the Council,
19th July 1940

The Formation of SOE

SUMMER 1940. FRANCE HAD FALLEN. The remnant of the British
Expeditionary Force had been evacuated from Dunkirk. Once the
threat of German invasion of Britain had receded, the need to take
the war to the enemy was acute. Yet the weakened British forces had
few options. One of these, irregular warfare, was dear to Winston
Churchill's heart. But we would be mistaken to imagine that SOE
sprang into life by demigod-like *fiat* from the great man to 'set Europe
ablaze'. It had a longer and more complicated history, intertwined
with that of the British military and intelligence 'communities' in
their belated transition from peace to war.

A tiny research section in the War Office's intelligence staff that
became known as Military Intelligence (Research) or MI(R)
comprised from 1938 the creative and imaginative Royal Engineers

officer Major J C F ('Jo') Holland and a typist. Holland had a relatively free hand, and his experience of action in Ireland and the Middle East, together with his fascination with guerrilla operations in general, led him to research irregular warfare.

At about the same time, SIS had formed a new 'Section D', importing Major Lawrence Grand, another Royal Engineers officer, to lead it. He was to investigate ways of weakening an enemy through sabotage, subversion and propaganda. The last of these involved some duplication, as the Foreign Office had also set up a more or less deniable unit at Electra House on Moorgate in London to explore propaganda options, led by Canadian newspaperman Sir Campbell Stuart and known either as 'EH' after the location or 'CS' after the name of the director.

Campbell Stuart and Grand were not told about each other's activities, but MI(R) and Section D compared notes and informally agreed that the former would focus on potentially acknowledgeable actions carried out in uniform, the latter on undercover work. Grand was authorised in March 1939 to initiate leafleting and sabotage in some of the occupied or threatened countries. He and Jo Holland, who had received similar orders on a 'Most Secret' basis, started to work together more closely, if rather stormily.

One of Jo Holland's colleagues, Colin Gubbins, drafted two pamphlets on guerrilla warfare and partisan leadership that, joined by a third on the use of explosives, would be widely distributed in English and over a dozen other languages during the subsequent years of the war.

The former pamphlet advised, for example, that 'the culminating stage of guerrilla warfare should always be to produce in the field large formations of guerrillas, well-armed and well-trained', but that 'in the early days of the war, guerrilla activities must, owing to the enemy's strength and to lack of support of the local population, be limited to acts of sabotage.[12]

---

[12] *The Art of Guerrilla Warfare*, Colin Gubbins, 1939.

Major-General Sir Colin Gubbins

Gubbins and another colleague, Tommy Davies, also prepared a training syllabus for individuals who could be called up ahead of general mobilisation. They set about recruiting and training them, partly through discussion courses for likely candidates at the St Ermin's Hotel near St James's Park in London. The plan was for them to travel on behalf of MI(R) with Military Missions to other countries, contacting local elements who might raise opposition in the event of German occupation.

St Ermin's Hotel

Gubbins himself was earmarked in July 1939 to lead the MI(R) element of a Mission to Poland. As intelligence reports predicted a German invasion of Poland by the end of August, Gubbins and a small team of hastily prepared officers – after a tortuous two-week, initiative-challenging journey via France, Malta, Egypt, Greece and Romania – arrived in Warsaw on 3rd September, two days after the invasion and six hours after Neville Chamberlain's declaration of war on Germany. Caught up in the confusion of the Polish defeat, his by now depleted party could do little to organise or support resistance, and Gubbins left Poland, at least better informed about the situation there. He was sent in November 1939 to liaise with the Polish and Czech military, now headquartered in Paris. However, he spent more time with Intelligence officers, with whom he discussed how Britain could help the fledgling Czech and Polish Resistance movements, particularly through supplying arms. In this, he learned the limits of cooperation with SIS, who jealously, and justifiably, guarded their existing contacts in those countries. MI(R) started to develop its own means of communications and supply.

During the 1939-40 'Phoney War', as a threat to Norway became more acute, MI(R) was ordered to plan for amphibious raids on the Norwegian coast. Jo Holland recalled Gubbins from Paris and put him in charge of planning for and training what became known as 'Independent Companies', forerunners of Commando forces. In May 1940, Gubbins was given command of *Scissorforce*, made up of four of these relatively autonomous units, tasked with harassing the German flanks and lines of communications in Norway. The story of the next three weeks, culminating in British evacuation from Norway, is complex and controversial, but Gubbins served with distinction and was awarded the Distinguished Service Order.

As Gubbins returned from Norway, however, German forces massed on the French side of the English Channel and prepared for *Unternehmen Seelöwe* (*Operation Sealion*), the invasion of Britain. Amid the desperate preparations to defend a vulnerable Britain against invasion, the most urgent form of irregular warfare seemed to be organising resistance in Britain itself. Jo Holland tasked Gubbins with building up a force of 'Auxiliary Units' that would challenge and demoralise the German occupiers. Intelligence officers, often with knowledge of the local area, secretly recruited local civilians to build hideouts in remote areas, training and equipping them to harass invading forces. The Auxiliary Units were of course never activated, but they were stood down only in 1944. Their life expectancy, if deployed, had been measured in hours and days rather than weeks and years. Many members took the secret of the Auxiliary Units to their graves decades later.

By May 1940, all of this research and action had given Jo Holland, Colin Gubbins and the rest of the small group a vast well of rapidly amassed knowledge of irregular warfare. On the 27th, Churchill's new coalition War Cabinet endorsed a proposal by the Chiefs of Staff, that planning, preparation and training for subversive operations should go ahead and that a new organisation was needed. The debate on whether this meant clandestine paramilitary operations or political subversion by anti-Fascist, i.e. left-wing, movements, and therefore whether the War Office, SIS or another agency should control the new entity, presaged tensions that would persist.

After the inevitable bureaucratic battles in Whitehall, Section D of SIS was subsumed in July 1940 into the new Special Operations Executive under Labour Minister Hugh Dalton's Ministry of Economic Warfare. MI(R) was disbanded in October 1940, its functions taken up by the new organisation. Ironically, SOE was called into life through a minute from Neville Chamberlain, who as Prime Minister had famously pursued appeasement with Hitler and who still held a senior ministerial position. Responsibility for propaganda was initially included, but later removed into a 'Political Warfare Executive'. So a relatively long period of research, staff planning and operational experience had informed and led to the formation of SOE in July 1940. Churchill's 'Set Europe ablaze' to Dalton did not come out of the blue.

A key motivation existed for forming the new organisation. At the time, it was widely assumed that the rapid German advance through the Low Countries and France had only been possible because prior subversion had undermined the governments. The assumption was mistaken, but it played to Hugh Dalton's enthusiasm for encouraging revolutionary movements in the occupied countries.

Dalton chose Sir Frank Nelson to lead the new secret organisation, headquartered in a messy collection of dispersed London office buildings, hotel rooms and apartments loosely centred on Baker Street. By November 1940, Dalton had won a battle with the Commander-in-Chief Home Forces to get Colin Gubbins into SOE. Gubbins joined as a brigadier, with responsibility for training and operations.

The structure of SOE was nothing if not fluid, but was broadly divided into operations – including training, signals and the highly independent and compartmentalised country sections – and those who provided facilities like weapons, supplies, finance and security. Cutting across the logic of this structure, though, were geographical complications; operations in the Middle East and Far East did not come within Gubbins' purview.

The best known of SOE's operations were organised by its country sections, for France, Poland, Norway, Yugoslavia, Czechoslovakia, the Netherlands and others in the European theatre. But the organisation aspired to and progressively gained a global reach. As the Japanese threat in Asia became more obvious, an Oriental Mission was secretly established with a base in Singapore, but the role was taken over by Delhi after Singapore fell to the Japanese. Cairo was the dysfunctional base for operations in the Balkans and the Middle East, while a small base to the west of Algiers (*Massingham*) was established in November 1942 for operations into Europe's 'soft underbelly'.

The sensitive area of liaison with the governments-in-exile in London also fell to SOE. Relations with the 'Fighting French' as they were generally called in 1941, were particularly tricky. At best, Charles de Gaulle reluctantly tolerated SOE activity in France, so when the SOE Oriental Mission was planning operations into colonial French Indochina in September 1941, London told them that 'de Gaulle knows of SOE activities in France and possibly Middle East but does not know of SOE activities in Far East. We do not wish him or his organisation to know of these activities.'[13]

Forming the Security Section

Much of the foregoing has been ably analysed by historians, but my particular focus is on those whose task was to keep SOE secure. The first step in doing so, in October 1940, was to form a Security Section.[14] It was led by wheelchair-bound Lieutenant-Colonel Edward Calthrop, whose SIS background fitted him for his ongoing role of liaison with that organisation. Edwin Whetmore was his deputy, tasked with recruitment. The Section remained small for several months, but included Captain E R W Breakwell and Major J D 'Jack' O'Reilly. O'Reilly, an enthusiastic 53-year-old Special Branch officer who had served in the Intelligence Corps in the 1914-18 war, was seconded from Scotland Yard for police liaison. He had served as a liaison officer with the French and Belgian police at various times during the 1920s and was adept at developing contacts.

As a better understanding of SOE's unique brand of warfare developed, the security needs expanded and became clearer, but they always included the physical security of the organisation's facilities in London, around the country and, eventually, around the world. The Section also vetted potential personnel and took steps to maintain SOE's cover.

At various stages of the war, SOE operated under a number of deliberately obscure cover names. Depending on who was asking, members of SOE might say they were from the Ministry of Economic Warfare, the Inter-Services Research Bureau, Headquarters Special Training Schools or MO1(SP). 'SOE' was used only by those in the know like the officers of MI5 or SIS. To prevent casual eavesdropping, simple everyday codes were used. Codes for countries included 12-land for Germany and 26-land for Norway.

---

[13] TNA HS 1/96, SO2 to OM, 14th September 1941.

[14] The Security Section was initially known as the D/T Section. In July 1941 it became a Directorate as D/CE.

I will return to some other aspects of the Security Section in the next chapter, but we are looking primarily at the group of men – the Field Security personnel – whose focus was on counter-intelligence. Nelson decided early that SOE would need a counter-espionage capability to protect the organisation externally from infiltration or observation and internally from betrayal or carelessness. They turned for this to the Army's newly reborn Intelligence Corps.

The Intelligence Corps

As Nicholas Van der Bijl recounts in *Sharing the Secret*, in the centuries before the Second World War, the need for military intelligence in support of British armies was only recognised once expeditionary operations were already under way. In peacetime, military intelligence specialists were under-appreciated and capabilities declined; having fulfilled the full range of intelligence tasks in the 1914-18 war, the Intelligence Corps was disbanded soon afterwards. In the 1930s, though, plans were in place, based on the 1922 Manual of Military Intelligence in the Field, to mobilise a small Intelligence Corps for the British Expeditionary Force, manned from 'the professional and literary classes' using a card index of potentially suitable individuals maintained for the purpose. Twenty-seven Field Security Sections, the workhorses of the Intelligence Corps, would deploy to France.

Putting these plans into practice, as the Nazi threat became clearer, required initiative, ingenuity and a measure of moral courage in the face of political unresponsiveness. Major Gerald Templer reviewed and revamped the neglected mobilisation plans for intelligence officers in late 1937. He started to identify likely candidates to be intelligence officers and warn them of their likely future fate. Together with Eric Shearer, a former Indian Army officer who was now a senior manager at the high-class food store Fortnum & Mason, he organised training courses in 1939 at the Royal United Services Institute on Whitehall and in Camberley. One student was quickly withdrawn from a course because of 'a rather adverse report';

he had been a Communist at Cambridge. This was Anthony Blunt, later an eminent art historian and confessed Soviet spy.[15]

Students paid their own course fees. Individuals with language skills in French and German were given a weekend course to become Field Security Officers. On 1st September 1939, as the German invasion of Poland was under way, Captain Arthur Sullivan arrived at Aldershot and started the *ad hoc* process of mobilising what would become the Intelligence Corps for war.

Once war had been declared on 3rd September, there was no longer any question of low-key, informal arrangements, although flexibility and initiative were still the watchwords. Field Security Sections and their harbour equivalents, Home Port Security Sections, reported to their places of duty. Within a few days of the start of the war, several Field Security Sections had disembarked at Cherbourg and were deploying in France as part of the British Expeditionary Force intended to deter a German attack. Others were receiving hurried training at the Field Security Wing at Mytchett to follow their comrades to France or to support formations remaining in Britain, quickly learning to deploy the flexibility and independence of thought that is essential to counter-espionage.

The relative quietude of the 'Phoney War' ensued, to be broken by the German invasion of Norway on 8th April 1940 and the catastrophic retreat from the Low Countries and France in the six weeks from 10th May. Meanwhile, preparations for re-establishing an Intelligence Corps culminated in King George VI giving authority to form the new Corps on 15th July. It took over responsibility for Field Security from the Military Police and eventually established the Field Security Training Centre at Winchester for Field Security NCOs; intelligence staff officers were trained at Matlock in Derbyshire and the Corps Headquarters staff were based at Pembroke and Oriel Colleges in Oxford. They would later consolidate and move to the great country house at Wentworth Woodhouse near Sheffield.

---

[15] *Mask of Treachery*, John Costello, 1988.

Counter-Espionage

In late 1940, SOE's Security Section consisted of only two or three people. They could set up a cloak of secrecy around the organisation, for instance by using its various cover names. They could vet potential members of SOE. But they could do little about a major issue: ensuring that the rapidly growing number of Special Training Schools around the country would remain secure. As an intelligence officer, Major Edwin Whetmore naturally thought of the Field Security concept. His letter to the Director of Military Intelligence requesting the establishment of three new Field Security Sections, to be SOE's counter-espionage arm, gained approval on 29th December 1940. The task was perhaps deliberately put in vague and innocuous terms, the men 'would be required to maintain observation on troops under instruction and to safeguard the internal and external security of our establishments'.[16]

They should be selected for their skills in foreign languages, to include French, German, Italian, Spanish, Dutch and Norwegian. This was in any case a characteristic of all Field Security personnel. Unlike many members of SOE, they were not recruited through an 'Old Pals' network but on the basis of their education and language ability. Although they served as humble lance-corporals, members of Field Security Sections were former schoolteachers, journalists or international businessmen. SOE had its pick of the bunch.

These first Sections – Nos 63, 64 and 65, consisting of thirty-eight non-commissioned officers – joined SOE in January and February 1941, and were commanded by Lieutenant Brian Walmsley, Lieutenant Thomas Brown and Captain William Glanville-Brown respectively. They were based at Brickendonbury Manor in Hertfordshire, the former SIS Section D training centre now to be known as Station XVII, at Guildford and at Kingston.

A Field Security Section consisted of an officer, thirteen NCOs and a driver, and was equipped for mobility with a truck and thirteen

---

[16] TNA HS 7/31.

motorcycles. The three SOE Sections were eventually put under the command of Peter Lee, a lieutenant in the Intelligence Corps. It was an unusual feature of life in SOE that military rank played little part in the positions individuals held. Rather, rank was often 'created' according to the needs of the post. Aonghais Fyffe, for instance, describing himself with excessive humility as a jumped-up lance-corporal and unable to command a wheelbarrow, was knowledgeable about the Scottish Highlands and was suddenly put in charge of No 6 Special Workshop School, the Inverlair 'cooler' that I describe in a subsequent chapter. Later in the war, SOE conformed a little more to military bureaucracy and sent more of those it wished to commission away to an Officer Cadet Training Unit.

Peter Lee, however, very quickly became a captain in order to be able to command the new Field Security Sections. He had been able to get an interview for SOE because on the previous evening one of Whetmore's captains 'had got roaring drunk at the Berkeley and told everyone what he did'.[17] After Lee's third and final interview in May 1941, in an attic office at 64 Baker Street, he was given the job and told by Whetmore to 'put up his third pip' because the job called for a captain. Up to that point, he had no idea what he was applying to join.

Lee got on well with his new boss. He later described Edwin Whetmore as charming, a person who could instantly establish rapport. Indeed, Whetmore was generally well liked in SOE. However, the *ad hoc* development of the Section, as SOE expanded and various avenues of security interest opened up, was regularised through a reorganisation in mid-1941. From then on, Whetmore appears to have had a personality clash with the senior leadership, especially with John Senter, the new Director of Security. Whetmore was seen as uncooperative under the new organisation and, his application to join SIS unsuccessful, was posted to Gibraltar.

A fourth unit, called No 2 Section and commanded by Captain Samuel Darby, was formed for SOE by the Intelligence Corps in

---

[17] IWM Oral History 7493, Peter Murray Lee.

September 1941 and SOE created its own fifth Section, No 84, in April 1942.

However, it became progressively clearer that securing the SOE training system and UK establishments was very different from the work of a normal Field Security Section attached to an Army formation or district. The idea of formed units was inappropriate for personnel who spent most of their time working independently or in small teams. Increasingly, the Field Security personnel were treated as a pool to be drawn from as necessary, and subsequent joiners came as individuals or in small groups to fill vacancies.

Geoffrey Spencer inspecting Field Security NCOs' motorcycles

'RTU'

Language skill was a requirement for Field Security personnel, but far from the only one. The men had to be reliable and trustworthy, able to operate independently for a period of thirteen weeks as they accompanied agents through the various stages of training and fit enough to participate alongside them. They might find themselves doing long runs in the Scottish Highlands, night sabotage exercises or parachute jumps into darkness.

Of the thirty-eight members of the first three Field Security Sections, eight were 'RTU'd': returned to their units for employment elsewhere. This does not necessarily mean that they were 'failures'. One lasted less than three weeks, so perhaps he was seen as unsuitable for the work or himself decided it was not for him. Others, though, stayed for several months or even for over a year. The reasons for their departure are often unclear. One of the later arrivals, who had been attacked and injured while serving in the Intelligence Corps in Mauritius, tragically died at his own hand some two weeks after taking up his SOE Field Security duties.

Another sad case was an infantry soldier who was recommended to Intelligence Corps officer Major Hardie Amies of SOE's Belgian Section as a potential agent. Before he could even start training, he was given compassionate leave to attend his wife, who was seriously ill in a Norfolk hospital. His wife died of kidney failure after a few weeks and the widower started candidate selection at Special Training School 4, hidden away at Winterfold House in Surrey. The training did not go well. Even allowing for the recent bereavement, the Commandant of STS 4 was unable to recommend this enthusiastic and determined student to work in-country. His timidity and lack of courage would make him a danger to others and himself. Amies withdrew him from training and, concerned about the security risk of releasing him back into the Army, suggested him to Peter Lee for Field Security duties, accompanying Belgian or French agents through their training. But after two weeks it became clear that he would not meet the requirements: RTU!

Other Field Security NCOs departed to take up duties in different areas outside SOE. Not all can be covered here, but a few give interesting insights into the secret world that was operating in parallel with 'The Racket', as SOE members sometimes called themselves.

The 'Other Service'

Relations between SOE and SIS at the political level were undoubtedly strained, perhaps inevitably given the potentially negative impact of subversion and sabotage on the quiet waters SIS naturally desired in which to fish for intelligence. Add to this the competition for resources like aircraft, and rivalry is almost guaranteed. The SIS leadership seemed to SOE to be constantly seeking ways to obstruct its operations. The assistant chief of SIS, Claude Dansey, is said to have gloated over the collapse through treachery of a major SOE network in France.

At the working level in the field, though, relations were often cooperative. SOE, like other elements of the Allied war machine, benefited from the intelligence product produced or coordinated by SIS, including sanitised access to Bletchley Park decrypts of German signals: the Most Secret *Ultra* product. In turn, SOE contributed intelligence gained as a by-product of its contacts in occupied countries. It may not always have been welcome. SOE agent Harry Rée's recollection is not verified, but he recounts having been offered drawings of the V2 rockets by a French engineer who had visited Peenemünde. Rée carried the drawings across the Swiss border to Bern and passed them to the SIS representative in the British Embassy, who retorted that outsiders should not get involved in this kind of thing.

Crossover of personnel also took place, even if those transferred sometimes represented a poisoned chalice. When D Section of SIS disbanded on the formation of SOE, several of its members were transferred to the new organisation. Others moved in the opposite direction. One person who joined SIS from SOE was Thomas Buck, who moved across in February 1944 and was commissioned. Not surprisingly for a case involving SIS, the circumstances are shrouded in mystery. Buck had joined SOE only six months earlier, so the award of the British Empire Medal in the New Year Honours of 1st January 1944 was a reward for his Intelligence Corps service before then, which included Field Security work in Iceland with 'C Force'.

More infamous individuals were transferred. Both Kim Philby and Guy Burgess, two of the 'Cambridge Spies', had come to SOE from Section D. Burgess was seen almost immediately by Colin Gubbins as a security risk because of his bohemian and alcoholic lifestyle, and Gubbins dismissed him in late 1940. Philby, with six or more years of experience as an unsuspected Soviet spy already under his belt, kept a lower profile and went on to lecture on propaganda at the SOE 'Finishing School' at Beaulieu. From there, he was recruited back into SIS in the autumn of 1941 and went on to serve his Soviet masters as a double agent for over twenty years.

CHAPTER 3

Politics and Subversion

'*A wise man in peace prepares for war.*'
Horace, *Satires*

Political Warfare

SOON AFTER SOE WAS FORMED, its propaganda arm, 'Special Operations 1', was hived off and amalgamated with units from the Ministry of Information and the BBC to become a new independent organisation, the Political Warfare Executive.[18] An existing secret department of the Foreign Office, the Political Intelligence Department, was used as cover for PWE, which made its home in the top floors of the BBC's Bush House.

SOE continued to provide PWE with support in getting agents into and back from the field and with training for its propaganda experts. Many propaganda operations were joint efforts. The training was initially done alongside the rudimentary training in propaganda given to SOE circuit organisers, but then became the focus of a new school at Woburn. Students learned to broaden their ideas on politics and social matters and to disseminate ideas effectively in a clandestine environment. Some of the Field Security personnel who are the subject of this book found their way into the new organisation. Among their number were David Alexander, George Harker and Frank Boyall.

---

[18] For simplicity, the term SOE is used throughout, but the special operations element of the organisation was initially known as SO2.

Just before PWE was formed, Corporal David Alexander was promoted from the ranks of No 65 Field Security Section to help set up the new organisation. This is probably the same Alexander who worked as an instructor at PWE's political warfare school and was later posted to Italy as the liaison officer for Political Warfare at 15th Army. As the Allies fought their way northwards, leaflets were produced and radio broadcasts transmitted, encouraging soldiers in the 'rump' Italian Fascist Army to desert.

George Harker was a late addition to SOE's 63 FSS, joining in the final days of 1941 to fill a vacancy. He was already well travelled. Born near Birkenhead, across the River Mersey from Liverpool, he had spent a great deal of his life in the Netherlands and had worked as a correspondent for United Press in Amsterdam two years before the war. Until early 1943, he worked as a Field Security NCO, presumably using his language knowledge to assist and report on Dutch agents in training. Somehow, he came to the attention of PWE, who wanted to use him as a wireless operator in Holland after the Allied occupation. The invasion was expected to take place by late 1943. SOE agreed to train Harker in Morse and radio procedures, did so, and transferred him to PWE.

In the comprehensive plan for supporting the eventual Allied invasion of the Low Countries, the political warfare aspects were designed to confuse the enemy and inform the population as to how they could best protect themselves, oppose the occupiers and aid the Allied invasion. Given the German counter-intelligence successes in Holland, of which more later, undercover deployments had to start more or less from scratch there in early 1944. However, a flourishing Dutch underground did exist, without much external support. PWE sent agents into Holland to contact and support the Dutch clandestine press, but it appears that Harker was not one of them. It is not clear whether he ever fulfilled the role for which he was transferred.

Unlike George Harker, Frank Boyall had joined SOE's Field Security Sections at their birth. Originally from Hull in the East Riding of Yorkshire, he had worked for six years as a ship broker in the Italian ports of Naples and Genoa, where he had learned Italian.

From 1932 until the outbreak of war, he managed the Fish Trade Information Bureau back in Hull; his wife Sadie stayed in the nearby village of Willerby when Frank went south to join up.

Frank did his Field Security training at Winchester over the winter of 1940-41 and was recruited into 65 Section when it formed in February. By the summer, he found himself promoted to 2nd lieutenant and wearing the 'pips' of a full lieutenant. An Italian-speaker was urgently needed. With his background, one could imagine him getting involved in maritime sabotage or becoming a conducting officer for Italian agents in training. His actual mission was much stranger. It is sometimes difficult in retrospect to decide how to describe SOE missions: imaginative concepts or hare-brained schemes. The same is true of PWE. The bizarre 'Italians in India' plan involved both organisations.

The fall of France had jolted Britain into seeking all possible ways to prosecute the war against Germany. Direct counter-attack on land in Europe was for the time being out of the question. Apart from aerial bombardment and anything that might bring America into the war, only indirect means like sabotage and propaganda remained open. To this end, SOE's predecessors had been searching among Italian internees on the Isle of Man and in the Auxiliary Military Pioneer Corps (later just the Pioneer Corps) for individuals who might form the kernel of a 'Free Italy' movement. The results were disappointing, and SOE started to look elsewhere. Surely the millions of Italian-Americans in the USA must include some convinced anti-Fascists. It was indeed the case.

The Mazzini Society, formed in 1940 in New York with Count Carlo Sforza as its figurehead, was the focus of American liberal anti-Fascism, among a divided Italian-American population that was generally more concerned about its position in American society. British undercover agents in New York from Sir William Stephenson's British Security Cooperation organisation proceeded to recruit volunteers from the Society to be trained for covert operations in Italy. With secret Canadian assistance and escorted by Royal Canadian Mounted Police, the first of them were smuggled into

Canada and shipped to Britain. These first twelve, of a planned force of 200, proved on arrival to be a severe disappointment. Many of them were unfit, older than expected, not suited to undercover work and unwilling to put on British uniform or be trained. Moreover, they had no intention of being saboteurs. They had apparently been led to expect that they would be employed on propaganda work to encourage Italian prisoners to join a Free Italy movement, under the control of the Mazzini Society rather than under British command.

Meanwhile, intense discussions had already taken place in Whitehall about developing the potential of Italian prisoners-of-war as a weapon against the Fascist regime. General Wavell's successes in North Africa and Abyssinia had yielded 160,000 Italian prisoners by March 1941. SOE decided to cut its losses, stop further recruitment in the USA and form this first group into a propaganda team to raise anti-Fascist feeling among Italian prisoners.

The chances of doing this in the Middle East, however, were slim. The dysfunctional nature of SOE Cairo, Wavell's opposition to the idea and the lack of potential interest among the POWs made it a lost cause. As a last resort, SOE decided to send the team to India, where 45,000 Italian POWs were imprisoned. The Foreign Office would not let them undertake direct propaganda, though. They were to investigate attitudes in the camps and see to the welfare of the prisoners, in the hope that a spontaneous Free Italy movement might be encouraged to arise.

This was where Frank Boyall came in. On 12th August 1941, he left Britain for India in the company of the depleted Mazzini Society group. He took over a group that was already riven with dissension. One of the two doctors in the group had been found to be disruptive and indiscreet; he was incarcerated on the Isle of Man, but the Mazzini Society was told that he was on a special mission. Another member had returned to the USA. As Special Operations 1 was becoming PWE, Boyall and the group were transferred to the newly formed organisation.

By the time they reached India in late September, the members of the group were metaphorically at each other's throats. Boyall reported that the group was so divided that the mission was a farce. The team had spent two months waiting in Calcutta for permission to enter India.

Things did not improve when they got to work, disguised as a medical mission but with their real purpose becoming more widely known through their indiscretions. Instructions to the leader, Lucio Tarchiani, came direct from his father at the Mazzini Society in New York *en clair*. In their visit to a camp in Bhopal, they had to retreat under stoning by prisoners who had recognised one of their number. After just four weeks among the POWs, the Mazzini group was disbanded in December 1941. But what could be done with the Italians in India?

Despite the desire of most of the group to return to America, the USA had entered the war and most of them were now classed as enemy aliens without passport or papers. They were kept in India. Some made a valuable contribution: Tarchiani was eventually commissioned into the Intelligence Corps and three others were enlisted as interpreters. The remainder continued to disrupt the efforts among the Italian POWs as they campaigned to be returned to the USA. PWE's mission in India continued to try to separate anti-Fascist prisoners from the remainder, but was eventually withdrawn in late 1943.

The Mazzini fiasco showed the dangers of working with untrained operatives whose motivation is unclear. But it was in some ways typical of SOE's (and PWE's) willingness to try almost any apparently promising idea. This one failed.

An Australian in the Far East

The most common image of SOE is of intrepid agents parachuting into occupied France, and Europe was certainly the main thrust of SOE's effort. However, the 1939-45 conflict was a world war. From its outset, SOE was an organisation with global ambitions. It could soon plausibly claim to have a worldwide political reach. One of the Field Security personnel, George Loftus Windred of 65 Section, quickly found himself part of that global story.

George Windred

Windred was born in April 1906 in Balmain, a suburb of Sydney, Australia. Like many of his Field Security colleagues, he was well educated. He attended the prestigious and academically selective Sydney High School and, recognised as highly intelligent, he graduated from the University of Sydney in 1929 with a Bachelor of Science degree in Agriculture. While at university, he gained some military experience with the Sydney University Regiment.[19] No doubt he paraded for the 1927 visit of the Duke of York, the future King George VI.

George Windred studied Chemistry, Botany, Zoology and Bacteriology, but his particular interest was insects. For his first job after graduation, he was employed by the Australia Council for Scientific and Industrial Research (CSIR),[20] specialising in the control

---

[19] The Australian equivalent of the University Officer Training Corps in the UK or the Reserve Officer Training Corps in the USA.

[20] Today the Commonwealth Scientific and Industrial Research Organisation, or CSIRO.

of insect pests. This organisation soon seconded him to the Government of the Dutch East Indies to work on solving the problem of the buffalo fly. During three years in Java, he had the opportunity to put his natural linguistic ability to work in learning Dutch and Malay, rare skills that he would later put to good use in SOE.

Sydney University parade 1927

In 1933, George returned from Java to work for CSIR in Australia's inland capital, Canberra, and there met his future wife, Gwendoline Graham, a well-travelled member of a prosperous Australian family whose sister, Lilian, an Oxford graduate, was also working at the research institution. In March of that year, though, George again left Australia, this time to fight against different insects. He took up a position with the Colonial Sugar Refining Company to find ways of battling sugar cane pests. This firm, headquartered just outside Sydney, had major sugar production facilities to the north, in Queensland, but also produced sugar in Fiji. George became the firm's Chief Scientist in Lautoka, Fiji, where Gwen joined him; they were married in Suva Cathedral in May 1934.

Fiji felt remote, and the pair escaped when they could. Gwen accompanied George on a five-week business trip to Hawaii in May/June 1935, sailing from Suva, Fiji, to Honolulu in the RMS *Niagara*. Five years later, the *Niagara* became infamous as the '*Titanic* of the Pacific', as she was sunk in Auckland's harbour entrance when leaving New Zealand, by a mine laid undetected by the German ship *Orion*. On board were 8 tons of gold bullion, *en route* from Britain to the USA as payment for urgently needed war material. In a remarkable deep-water diving feat in 1941, New Zealand and Australian salvage divers recovered the bulk of the gold, amounting to 555 gold bars.

Gwen Windred

In Hawaii, George and Gwen shopped for clothes in Japanese shops, but they also viewed the US fleet at Pearl Harbor, not knowing how it too would become infamous, its name recognised worldwide for the Japanese attack that brought the USA into the war.

By 1935, George was starting to make something of a name for himself in his specialised academic field. He was elected a Fellow of the Royal Entomological Society in March of that year and gave a paper at a conference in Brisbane in August. But this was not his real ambition. He was more interested in the theatre.

During his time in Fiji, George had organised the Amateur Dramatic Society and the experience had awakened his real ambition: to be an actor. Thanks to Gwen's family money, he was able to realise this dream, at least for a time. When war intervened, he would take up a different kind of acting.

Clearly George saw greater opportunities to fulfil his thespian dream in 'the old country' than in Fiji or even in Australia, because he and Gwen decided to relocate to London. No administrative barriers existed; George, his wife and indeed his parents, born in colonial Australia, were all British citizens. Gwen, pregnant with their first child, went first, sailing via New Zealand and the Panama Canal, and settled in London.

Their son Richard was born in London in July 1936. George travelled from Fiji via the USA, arriving at Southampton from New York on the Cunard White Star Line's RMS *Berengaria* two weeks after the birth and, no doubt, catching a fast train to London. He spent a few weeks with his family in London, but then returned to Fiji to work for the sugar company for a few more months. In May 1937, after visiting relatives in Australia, he sailed from Sydney Harbour for the long sea journey to Southampton, arriving on 20th June.

On settling in England, George enrolled for a one-year drama course at the Embassy School of Acting, based at the Embassy Theatre in Swiss Cottage, North London. Starting with walk-on parts, he gradually built up his experience and prominence on the stage. As well as the school's own productions, he took on roles like that of a Communist prisoner in Stephen Spender's anti-Fascist drama *Trial of a Judge*. Like most struggling young actors, George was not instantly catapulted to West End stardom. Spender's play was staged in the Unity Theatre in the down-at-heel Kings Cross area of London. Tickets cost one shilling, and the 100-seat theatre was generally only half-full.

George built a new circle of friends, including Richard Wordsworth – great-great-great-grandson of the poet – a fellow student at drama school who became a well-known Shakespearean actor. Towards the end of his drama training, George joined the touring company founded the previous year by (later Sir) Donald Wolfit, often called the last great actor-manager. Famously put down by actress Hermione Gingold in the quip '[Laurence] Olivier is a *tour de force*, but Wolfit is forced to tour', Wolfit took his Shakespeare productions around the country. George appeared in several of these, taking the roles of Rosencrantz in *Hamlet*, Conrad in *Much Ado about Nothing* and Lorenzo in *The Merchant of Venice*. In the Christmas production of *Alice in Wonderland* in Stratford-upon-Avon, George played the Dodo and the Knave of Hearts. According to the *Gloucestershire Echo* of 6th December 1938, in Wolfit's touring production of *The Merchant of Venice* on the previous evening:

> George Windred and Sarah Fox ... were Lorenzo and Jessica, for whom Shakespeare created one of the most tender love scenes of all times. This, the moonlit introduction of the last scene, was lingeringly and sensitively done.

Meanwhile, signs of the danger of war were becoming more ominous, even on the stage. In March 1939, Gwen and George queued at the Apollo Theatre for tickets to see the Pulitzer Prize-winning comedy *Idiot's Delight* by Robert Sherwood. The play, starring Robert Massey, imagined British, German, American and French guests trapped together in an Italian hotel as a European war loomed; Gwen found it 'most amusing and horridly realistic at the same time'.[21] Tension grew. Later that year, Neville Chamberlain flew twice to Munich to negotiate with Adolf Hitler.

While the Prime Minister was in Germany, the British newspapers were full of the crisis. War preparations began. Gwen and George went to Chelsea Town Hall to be fitted for gas masks. Gwen felt it her duty to take 2-year-old Richard away from danger, packed a trunk and – against George's wishes – caught a train to Devon to stay with a relative. When Chamberlain returned on 30th September 1938 waving

---

[21] Quotes by Gwen Windred are from her private diaries.

the famous piece of paper representing the agreement with Hitler, the population did not have our benefit of hindsight. According to Gwen, there was 'wild enthusiasm in London'. The agreement allowed German occupation of the Sudetenland of western Czechoslovakia and agreed peace between Germany, France and Britain. 'The Czechs had to give in for the peace of the world', wrote Gwen. It was 'heavenly to have the crisis over'.

Until 1939, George, Gwen and Richard lived in an apartment near Onslow Square in Kensington, London. As war approached, however, life in London appeared increasingly risky, and Gwen took Richard back to Devon. By February 1940, the German threat to England appeared to have been exaggerated and Gwen moved to a rented house near Sevenoaks in Kent, closer to London: and to George. Meanwhile, George had given up the theatre and moved into a rented room; he was working as a Training Officer in the Air Raid Precautions organisation, based at a Stretcher Party Depot in South Kensington.

On 10th May 1940, the Phoney War ended abruptly. The German invasion of the Low Countries and France was swift. The British Expeditionary Force was encircled; its evacuation from Dunkirk was completed on 4th June. Ten days later, German troops entered Paris. Southern England was suddenly in real danger.

On 15th June, with German troops on the French coast, Gwen and George had a serious talk about their prospects. George felt that their only option was for Gwen to take Richard to safety in Australia and to stay there until the future became clearer. The first air raid warning, presaging what we now know as the Battle of Britain, came on 25th June and put the seal on their decision. They were more fortunate than many others in England; they had a safe haven available to them. A few weeks later, Gwen and Richard embarked at Liverpool in the SS *Ceramic*, bound for Sydney. It would be an eventful voyage.

The ship had reached the South Atlantic when, in the early hours of the morning of 11th August 1940, she was accidentally rammed by a cargo vessel. Two blasts from the ship's siren were followed by two terrific crashes, as the ship quivered from end to end. For security reasons, both ships had been sailing without navigation lights. Despite the large hole ripped in her starboard side, the *Ceramic* stayed afloat and was towed to South Africa for repairs. Gwen and Richard, with nearly 300 other passengers, were transferred by lifeboat to the P&O liner RMS *Viceroy of India*. Two days later, they arrived in Capetown, where they had to wait another six weeks for onward passage to Australia. They travelled there in the SS *Themistocles* and disembarked at Sydney on 1st November.

After staying with Gwen's mother and then her sister until the end of the year, they settled near Hobart, Tasmania, where Gwen made a life for herself and her son in the remote hamlet of Fern Tree on the road to Mount Wellington: growing vegetables, preserving fruit, playing bridge with neighbours. Richard caught a bus each day to Hutchins, a boys' school in Hobart. Gwen kept in touch with the rest of the world through family letters, often weeks in transit, and two-month-old copies of *Punch* and *The Listener*. She and Richard remained in Tasmania until late 1944. They were as far as they could be from the war's dangers – but also from George.

In September 1940, George joined the Field Security service, by then part of the Intelligence Corps. He trained at Winchester and Matlock, and was initially posted to No 55 Field Security Section, attached to 6th Armoured Division. However, when Edwin Whetmore requested Field Security personnel from the Intelligence Corps with language skills, Lance-Corporal Windred was a prime candidate. He joined SOE's 65 FSS, based in Kingston upon Thames in Surrey, on 24th February 1941. His stay in the Section was even shorter than that of Frank Boyall.

As a speaker of Dutch, George was at first sent to accompany Dutch agents on their training courses, getting to know them and reporting weekly to Peter Lee on their reliability. When called upon, he carried out practice interrogations in Dutch. The Dutch Section, under Mr R V Laning, had only existed since just before Christmas 1940 and was still finding its feet in a process that culminated in enemy control of almost all Dutch SOE agents in what the Germans called the *Englandspiel* – the 'England Game'. George cannot have made a great contribution to securing the Dutch Section, as he almost immediately left it, having been 'specially selected for a post of great confidence', according to his formal report on discharge from 'Service with the Colours'. The discharge was a formality allowing his commissioning as a 2nd lieutenant on 3rd April 1941, after just six months in the Army and having reached the dizzy heights of lance-corporal as a soldier. He had 'certain qualifications which fit him for service as an Officer in this Organisation'. As ever, SOE was pragmatic in its attitude to commissioned rank.

The 'post of great confidence' was connected as much with his experience in the Far East as his language ability, for he was destined for SOE's newly formed Oriental Mission. Having briefly worked alongside Dutch SOE agents, George was rapidly trained as an agent himself. He was recognised as a tough Australian (even though his pre-war acting experience had not left him with much of an Australian accent). Despatched to Arisaig in Scotland and to two other SOE training schools, he learned how to sabotage railways and other infrastructure and was trained in the art of propaganda. By mid-May, he was on his way to join the Oriental Mission, which was based in Singapore under the cover of the Ministry of Economic Warfare. The requirement to prepare for subversive action, in the context of an imminent Japanese threat, was a politically controversial topic in the Far East.

Planning for the Oriental Mission had started in late 1940. Its ostensible role was to collect economic and industrial intelligence throughout the Far East. Its secret purposes were to organise subversive propaganda and covert operations 'in certain circumstances which may shortly develop', for which it was placed under the control of the Commander-in-Chief Far Eastern Command. However, SOE's concepts developed for Europe, and the experience so far gained there, did not translate easily to Asia. In contrast to European guerrilla movements determined to disrupt the German occupation, resistance in the Far East was as likely to oppose British, Dutch and French colonial masters as the Japanese. Physical difficulties faced SOE, too. Operating conditions in the jungle were more severe, the chance of white faces passing unnoticed was more remote, and distances were greater than in Europe.

The leader of the Oriental Mission, former ICI China manager Valentine Killery, had immense difficulty setting the organisation up after he and its senior officers arrived in Singapore in April-May 1941, constrained by shortage of time and 'much local misunderstanding and opposition from British authorities'.[22]

The Mission set up a training school on the south coast of Singapore Island, known as Special Training School 101 and modelled on the SOE schools in the UK. But it focused mainly on training Europeans, having been prohibited by British authorities from recruiting 'orientals' from the target countries. George Windred arrived in Singapore to find the Oriental Mission working against the clock to set up 'stay-behind' parties in the Far Eastern theatre in the event of Japanese occupation.

George had travelled 'westabout' to reach the other side of the globe. He left the port of Liverpool on 16th May 1941 in the SS *Port Sydney* for a hazardous transatlantic journey. Also on board when George arrived in New York on 2nd June was a British diplomat, a survivor rescued from a sinking ship, probably in the same convoy. The danger of U-boat attack was ever-present.

In New York, George would have contacted the small organisation at 630 Fifth Avenue led by Sir William 'Little Bill' Stephenson, the clandestine services' representative in the USA with responsibility for all SOE activity in the Americas. Stephenson's quiet contribution to turning US public opinion away from isolationism in 1940-41 was, according to SOE historian M R D Foot, 'probably the most important thing that SOE ever did'.[23]

George was travelling undercover as a civilian biologist, his Army commission quietly concealed. Despite SOE's obsession with secrecy, he used his own name, and was fortunate that Japanese Intelligence

[22] TNA HS 7/111 History of SOE Oriental Mission May 1941 - March 1942.
[23] *SOE: an outline history of the Special Operations Executive 1940-1946*, M R D Foot, 2008, p. 247.

never got around to reading the *London Gazette* of 6th May 1941, where the award of the King's Commission and his connection with the Intelligence Corps were recorded. He travelled to the west coast by the transcontinental train *The Chief* and departed from Los Angeles on 13th June for the five-day sea voyage to Honolulu. Unlike his vacation trips from Fiji to Hawaii, this visit only allowed him a two-night stay.

Pan Am Clipper poster, 1930s

On the 20th, he travelled by Pan Am *California Clipper* – the new transpacific flying boat service – to Singapore, alighting on the way at Midway, Wake, Guam and Manila. As well as carrying passengers in luxury to the Far East, the Clippers provided the most reliable wartime mail service between Britain and Australia.

With our current high-speed communications – emails, WhatsApp, FaceTime etc – it is easy to forget that letters could take months to arrive. The censorship process added to the delay, to frustration and to marital tension. For the short time George was based in Singapore, however, he and Gwen were able to communicate with a delay of only a week or two.

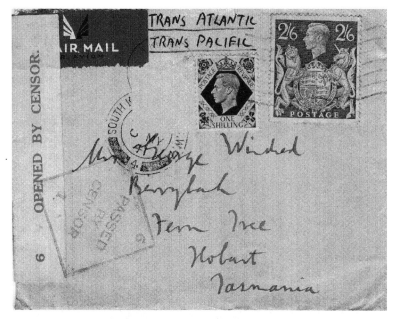

Letter from George in Britain, sent via the USA, the safest route

In Singapore, George maintained his cover as a biologist, working in the College of Medicine on research into controlling destructive pests in stored goods. Under this guise, he participated in the colonial social life of dinner parties, plentiful food and copious drink – often at Raffles Hotel – which continued oblivious of the looming Japanese threat. Gwen knew something of his real work, but he was relieved that other members of the family thought that entomology was the passion of his life. Some acquaintances, with a more romantic frame of mind gained from novels, saw the point much too quickly for his peace of mind, and he had the greatest difficulty in converting them to the more mundane interpretation.

He used the entomology cover for his first mission. Soon after his arrival in Singapore, he was sent to different parts of Malaya to assess the qualities of various people to recruit and direct 'stay-behind' parties, who would be trained at STS 101 and returned to Malaya. George Windred's time in Malaya was not how we usually picture an SOE mission: parachute drops or Lysander landings at dead of night, small boats sliding silently into deserted coves. Malaya, and the Straits

Settlements that included the island of Singapore, were under indirect or direct British control and George was free to travel. He did so in an SS Jaguar sports car, driving from Kuala Lumpur to more remote jungle areas like Ipoh, Bentong and Mentakab, coasting down hills to save fuel and using the car's excellent handling capabilities on hairpin bends.

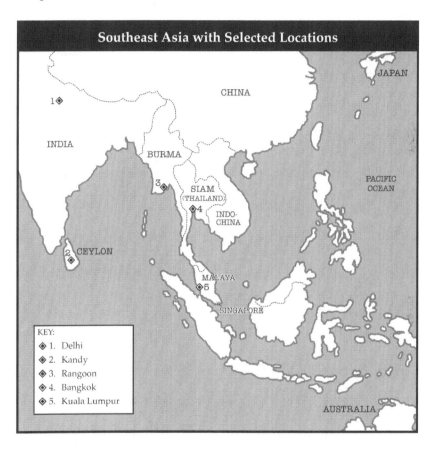

He was mostly working with expatriate rubber plantation managers, both to organise the 'stay-behind' parties and to investigate how supplies of rubber, a significant war resource, could if necessary be disrupted. When in Kuala Lumpur, he stayed with Hugh Smith, statistician at the Rubber Research Institute, whose wife Alice founded a home school after the war that developed into a major expatriate school. Following a predecessor's failure, George Windred was the only agent preparing Malaya for potential subversion against the Japanese.

On the basis of Windred's reconnaissance, the Mission submitted a proposal for subversive action in Malaya by SOE, but it was rejected following opposition by Lieutenant-General Arthur Percival, General Officer Commanding Malaya, perhaps piqued that he had not been consulted in advance. Soon after the start of the Japanese war, however, the military requested urgent subversive action and it was hurriedly implemented by the Oriental Mission.

A demolition party, led by the commander of STS 101 and using intelligence gathered by George Windred and others, destroyed an electric light works and tin smelter at Butterworth and fuel dumps at Penang and Kuala Lumpur. By this time the 'stay-behind' parties, amounting to about forty newly commissioned British officers and over 100 Chinese Communists, had to be infiltrated across enemy lines, severely restricting their effectiveness.

Some of these agents were able to escape after the fall of Singapore and were the catalyst for later operations in Malaya by SOE's India Mission. The Oriental Mission had laid the foundations of organised anti-Japanese guerrilla warfare, by groups of both Malay and Chinese origin. Simultaneously, the agents made arrangements with local villagers for escape routes for British troops cut off by the Japanese advance. Several thousand soldiers escaped via the routes initially laid down by SOE.

Charles Cruickshank, in *SOE in the Far East*, suggests that, had time and permission existed to set up 'stay-behind' parties and develop armed resistance, as planned by the Oriental Mission on the basis of George Windred's reconnaissance, Japanese lines of communication could have been threatened. Allied defence against the Japanese advance would have been more effective, and the outcome might have been very different.[24]

---

[24] *SOE in the Far East*, Charles Greig Cruickshank, 1983, p. 249.

Into Siam

After his work in Malaya, George Windred's next mission was in Thailand.[25] The degree of support or opposition in Asia for SOE's Oriental Mission was patchy, depending on personalities in the different countries. Thailand was an ostensibly neutral country and Sir Josiah Crosby, British Minister in Bangkok, was trying to maintain a diplomatic relationship with the Thai Government. He gave this priority over clandestine preparations to oppose Japan militarily, even though, in response to infiltration by Japanese military officers in civilian guise, he had earlier in 1941 recommended sending British officers disguised as civilians. During the summer, the legal implications of insertion of soldiers in civilian clothes were debated. Deployment of larger numbers – Independent Companies of the type used in the Norway campaign – was considered, but the role was eventually left to SOE's Oriental Mission.

Killery, increasingly frustrated by Crosby's resistance to his initiatives and impatient with the political caution of the diplomats in London, decided in mid-November 1941 to send George Windred to Bangkok. To date, only European expatriates had been recruited. Windred's task would be to recruit Thai individuals and further expatriates for resistance to the Japanese, with a view to training them in demolition work at the SOE school in Singapore. In doing so, Killery was acting not only without the knowledge of Crosby but also without informing his own agent already in place in Thailand, who he thought was not sufficiently aggressive.

Captain Windred, as he now was, travelled to Bangkok posing as a journalist, with forged credentials purporting that he worked for Benn Brothers of Fleet Street, a publisher of technical journals and the Blue Guide series of travel guides. Killery advised SOE in London that Windred would send authentic articles direct to the publisher,

---

[25] The terms Siam/Siamese and Thailand/Thai were both used at the time, and had political connotations. Not for political reasons but to aid understanding for the 21st Century reader, I will use the latter unless referring to a title used at the time, such as 'Siam Country Section'.

which Benn could publish if they wished, and asked Baker Street to ensure that the company would confirm his credentials if requested to do so.

Meanwhile, SOE in London vacillated about whether Crosby should be informed of Windred's presence and whether the visit was 'exploratory' or would involve 'recruitment' or even 'action'. The whole controversy, made worse by London and Singapore 'talking past each other' through delayed telegraphic communications, was in hindsight like Nero's apocryphal 'playing the fiddle while Rome burned'. It was quickly overtaken by events. The Japanese entered Thailand during the night of 7th/8th December 1941.

George Windred, incommunicado in Bangkok and oblivious to the controversy about his presence there, pressed on with recruiting Resistance operatives. In the short time he had available, he may have been able to achieve a little in central and northern Thailand. In southern Thailand, an SOE network had already been built up with the purpose of disrupting tin mining.

The Far East Command had in August 1941 proposed a plan, *Operation Matador*, to deploy British troops into southern Thailand to deter and if necessary defend against a Japanese attack on Malaya. However, resources were not available and it was never implemented. As part of this plan, SOE agents were to disrupt the Japanese advance by demolition of bridges and railways, by taking over Phuket airfield and by guerrilla warfare against Japanese units.

As it turned out, the Commander-in-Chief's reluctance to 'interfere' in a neutral country overrode the urgency of the situation. The warning signal to activate the SOE agents in Thailand was not given until a few hours after the Japanese had invaded at various points in southern Thailand, less than twenty-four hours after their surprise attack on the American fleet at Pearl Harbor.

The SOE agents were able to disable a few of Thailand's tin mines, destroy an electricity power station, cut some telephone lines and occupy Phuket airfield for two days. It was too little, too late. They had expected Thai forces to offer at least some opposition to the Japanese, but Thai resistance lasted only a few hours. Subsequently, the Japanese invaders demanded and received cooperation. Some SOE agents were evacuated with fleeing European civilians and some killed, the remainder arrested by the Thai police and interned. George Windred, not known to be a British officer, was among the latter group. He was captured on 12th December 1941.

Interned

Japanese forces used Thailand as a base to advance westwards into Burma and southwards towards Malaya and Singapore. Quickly establishing air supremacy and neutralising naval opposition by sinking HMS *Prince of Wales* and HMS *Repulse*, by the end of January 1942 they had driven Allied ground forces out of Malaya. Under aerial bombardment and amphibious assault, the defences of Singapore held out for a further two weeks. Lieutenant-General Percival surrendered the Allied garrison on 15th February 1942.

By then, the officers of the Oriental Mission had escaped from Singapore. Seen in London as a failure, the Mission was disbanded and its staff dispersed, many of them to SOE's India Mission. Valentine Killery, who had been in Java when Singapore fell, escaped from there to Australia, where he played a key role in the establishment of the Australian equivalent of SOE.

In Bangkok, after a week of confusion, the Japanese agreed that the Thai Government could look after the civilian internees. Although Thailand had sided with the Japanese, it remained an independent state. About 200 British, American and Dutch internees were rounded up by the Thai police and taken in trucks to the Thammasat University of Moral and Political Sciences, near the Chao Phraya River. The students had been moved out.

Internment by the Thai as a civilian represented a far less unfortunate fate than becoming a prisoner of war, or even a civilian internee, under the Japanese, the horrors of which have become well-known. The infamous Thai-Burma Railway was constructed by over 180,000 Asian forced labourers and 60,000 Allied prisoners forced to work in conditions of starvation and disease. Over 10,000 POWs and ten times as many Asian slave workers died.

The Commandant of the civilian internment camp, a Thai Customs officer who had been called up as an Army officer, was a kind individual already known to many of the internees. He allowed them to organise themselves as they wished, provided behaviour was good. They all had friends outside the camp and received frequent visits. They were able to contact Swiss expatriates to borrow money, in order to make their life more comfortable.

Some of the more senior managers of tin mines and other companies found it difficult to adjust from their luxurious lifestyle, with servants, to living in dormitories. George did not find this a problem. For the first six months, though, food was basic and not plentiful. The diet was inadequate to maintain health and many cases of beri-beri and scurvy presented themselves. Later, the internees were able to pay to bring in Chinese cooks and make their own catering arrangements.

In 1942, when the possibility arose of an internee exchange, SOE was asked by the Foreign Office to nominate any interned agents it wished to recover. George Windred was consistently top of the priority list, but SOE was very concerned that his cover as a civilian should never be compromised. He was not released. About 100 American internees were repatriated and later a smaller number of British. They were transported by Japanese ship to Lourenço Marques (now Maputo) in Mozambique, where they were exchanged for Thai internees.

The guards in Bangkok were from the Thai Army, but normally stayed outside the camp. Within the perimeter, internees organised themselves, with a camp committee whose chairman liaised with the Commandant. The Japanese inspected the camp infrequently. After the first few weeks, they did not directly check on who was present. The Thai guards always gave warning of Japanese visits, allowing internees to hide any items that would arouse suspicion. After the first year, internees were occasionally permitted to leave the camp, for instance to visit a dentist or even to have lunch with friends.

Although the Thai Government had little choice but to cooperate with the Japanese, many of the Thai people were sympathetic to the

Allied cause and supported those in the camp. Two internees were able to acquire a clandestine radio receiver with headphones, passed to them over the fence from a river boat while others were watching a concert. This was kept secret from most of the inmates, but it was possible to transcribe the main points of the BBC Eastern Service broadcasts and distribute them to trusted individuals around the camp. Much of the content was written and read by author George Orwell, a BBC employee at the time.

Even though they were cautious and did not let the news spread too widely, the camp's inmates gained a reputation with the Thai of being fully up to date. Through their many outside contacts, the internees heard that conditions on the Burma railway were appalling. Many of them raised money from Chinese traders on personal guarantee, to be paid back after the war, and sent medical supplies and other aid to the suffering POWs, establishing a clandestine riverborne courier service between the internment camp and the POW work camp.

Through their radio receiver, the internees kept up to date with war news. When they heard about the D-Day landings in France, it was clear that the tide of the war was turning. Allied bombing raids on Bangkok increased. The camp was situated worryingly close to a Thai submarine and two destroyers moored in the river and not far from one of Bangkok's railway stations.

After the camp was hit by bombs in March 1945, the internees were relocated, against vigorous Japanese protest. Backed by the Swiss Consul, they made representations to the Camp Commandant and were moved to a safer location in another college campus by the name of Vajiravudh, upriver and further from the centre of Bangkok. The Japanese never visited the new camp, which was co-located with, but separate from, a camp for POWs. Social contact between the two camps was relatively free, and the Thai Camp Commandant was in touch with either OSS or SOE, or both, through Free Thai operatives parachuted into Thailand.

Allies of a Kind

The political situation in Thailand was far from straightforward. Although an independent country, Thailand had been highly dependent on trade with the British colonies that almost surrounded it. A relatively liberal government had been overthrown by a Fascist-style military regime under Phibun Songkhram. It was this latter that, in the absence of a security guarantee from Britain – itself not credible without US support – tried to judge how much it must accommodate Japanese demands.

Ultimately, the Thai Government cooperated with the Japanese, allowing free passage for Japanese troops for their advance on Burma and Malaya, and in January 1942 declared war on the USA and Britain. Britain responded in kind, but the USA chose to ignore the declaration and treat Thailand as Japanese-occupied territory.

Thus American and British political attitudes towards Thailand differed. The US State Department, like China suspicious of Britain's post-war colonial ambitions, showed more sympathy to the Thai plight as an 'ally' of Japan, albeit under coerced occupation, than did the British Foreign Office. SOE tried to persuade London to soften its line and assist Thai attempts to undermine the Japanese, so that American and British clandestine organisations could work together. There was a back story. SOE had played a major part in the formation of OSS and the training of its operatives. In the latter years of the war, OSS leader General Bill Donovan and his staff were keen to shake off the 'junior partner' image.

The uncoordinated approach had its price. Thailand had a substantial underground movement willing to resist Japan, led by a political rival of Phibun, Pridi Phanomyong. Pridi made tentative and sporadic contact with SOE and OSS in India and China, and with Free Thai movements in the UK and USA. Each of the two Allies had recruited Free Thai volunteers – many of them Thai who had been studying at British or American universities – for infiltration by submarine or parachute into the country.

Statue of Pridi Phanomyong at Thammasat University

Following the fall of Singapore and dissolution of the Oriental Mission, responsibility for Thailand rested with SOE's India Mission, led by Colin Mackenzie, through its Siam Country Section. Although operations in Thailand were not expected for at least eighteen months, Mackenzie thought forward planning essential. He put work in hand to identify officers in the British Forces with experience of Thailand, many of whom had trekked out of the country when the

Japanese arrived. They would work alongside the Free Thai and Chinese agents who were being recruited and trained.

The Mission was initially based at Meerut, near Delhi in India, but from November 1944 was in Kandy, Ceylon (today's Sri Lanka). By then it was designated 'Force 136' and was much more closely integrated with the military than the Oriental Mission had been.

From September 1943, the subversive and intelligence activities of SOE, OSS and SIS in the Far East were at least in theory coordinated – and their competing demands arbitrated – by a division of Admiral Lord Louis Mountbatten's Southeast Asia Command. In effect, though, Force 136 and OSS ran separate and uncoordinated operations in Thailand, characterised by intrigue, suspicion and duplication of activities.

Admiral Lord Louis Mountbatten, Singapore, September 1945

The Thai, particularly after a change of government in August 1944, were cooperating with the Japanese just enough to prevent them taking over direct control of the country. Meanwhile, substantial elements of the Thai police and army had followed Pridi's lead and joined the secret anti-Japanese movement. Partially armed guerrilla forces were in effective control of northern Thailand. Despite SOE's wish to cooperate with OSS in supporting Pridi, the American organisation – or at least several of its key officers – harboured an almost paranoid suspicion of British motives and placed limits on how closely it was willing to work with SOE. It is hard to escape the conclusion that OSS's single-minded and secretive pursuit of an American political relationship with Pridi caused a lost opportunity, namely cooperative Allied training and equipping of the Free Thai opposition in-country. Nevertheless, SOE bore its share of the blame for the inter-Allied hostility.

By mid-1945, though, the Resistance forces had become stronger, involving the Thai army, the police force, civilian volunteers and a substantial guerrilla force being trained by Force 136 and the OSS. Pridi – code name *Ruth* – was communicating separately with OSS and Force 136. However, he had to be cautious about taking military action against the Japanese. Too early an uprising would lead to full occupation by reinforced Japanese forces and make an Allied attack more difficult. Pridi was asked to wait for the go-ahead from the Supreme Allied Commander, Admiral Mountbatten, who:

> realised the difficulty [Pridi] had to hold these forces in leash, but ... had also to keep in mind the tremendous danger of a premature move which would bring down crushing Japanese counter-action.[26]

Moreover, action in Thailand at the right time could divert the Japanese from opposing a potential Allied attack in Malaya. The word never came. Following the US use of atomic weapons against Hiroshima and Nagasaki, Japan's surrender was announced on 15th August 1945.

How aware George Windred, in the Bangkok internment camp, was of the high-level Thai political opposition to the Japanese, and

---

[26] Speech by Admiral Mountbatten at the City Livery Club, quoted in The Times, 18th December 1946.

what part he may have played in it, is not certain. It may be that, in the transfer of responsibility for Thailand from the disbanded Oriental Mission to the India Mission and Force 136, his presence in Bangkok was simply forgotten. Through the Free Thai Movement, however, Force 136 were very much aware of what was happening in-country, especially in Bangkok. George Windred's character and his mission make it very unlikely that he would simply have mouldered in the camp. Inmates had a great deal of outside contact, and George is likely to have played a full part in everything that was going on.

George gave no clues. Reports of his activity in the camp focus on his training of a volunteer Red Cross team in first aid and similar skills, his cooking skills over a charcoal brazier, or his production of Shakespeare plays: *A Midsummer Night's Dream* and *The Merchant of Venice*. He appears to have received no family news, even though Gwen wrote him a dozen or more letters via the Red Cross. Yet the internees had sympathetic Thai guards, some freedom of movement and good communications with the outside world in Bangkok. Moreover, three downed American airmen and six OSS-trained Free Thai agents were brought to the camp in May and December 1944.

Gathering intelligence and passing it back to Allied forces was an important role for SOE, OSS and their Free Thai partners. George would have been careful about revealing his identity as a British officer, even to fellow internees, but family sources suggest that he was able to support intelligence-gathering through a Thai network he organised from the camp.

Although stage productions continued and he gave voice coaching and applied make-up for the amateur actors, he seems to have involved himself very little in social matters but kept his time free for more important activities. He kept his counsel, being recognised in the camp as 'quiet but extraordinarily well informed'. He never knew how much of his information on Japanese troop dispositions ever reached the Allies. By late 1944, though, the Allies were receiving information of a high standard via a widespread and regular intelligence system. Despite his constraints, George Windred appears to have played a role in this.

The demarcation in other theatres between the intelligence role played by SIS and SOE's subversive activities was much less marked in the Far East. SOE was stronger on the ground than SIS, in Thailand as in other Asian countries, and used these resources to fill a vacuum in intelligence-gathering. The demarcation did not exist in the American equivalent; organisationally, OSS covered both roles.

The Australian Connection

Australian soldiers, sailors and airmen were active in all theatres: North Africa, the Italy campaign, the Far East. Australia itself may have seemed geographically remote from the war, but the risk of Japanese attack or invasion was real. Even in distant Tasmania, Air Raid Precautions were organised. Gwen and Richard were issued with respirators and trained in their use. Later, Gwen trained in Hobart as an ARP telephonist.

For many months, Gwen had no idea whether George was alive or dead. She had received a cable from him, sent in Bangkok on 6th December 1941, two days before the Japanese occupation, so she knew he was in mortal danger. Given the clandestine nature of his mission, this was truer than she realised.

Not until 31st July 1942 did she receive notification from the Australian Red Cross, Tasmania Division, that the International Red Cross in Geneva had a postcard signed by George: 'I am detained in Protection Camp Thailand. Am well.' These Red Cross cards held standard wording, with options to 'delete where inapplicable'. It had been signed by George six months earlier, on 16th January 1942.

In November, Gwen received the physical card written in January and started to receive news of George from Dutch and Australian internees who had been repatriated. On 24th November, Gwen received a letter forwarded by her mother, from the Belgian Superintendent of the Bangkok Power Station, Monsieur Delacroix, who was free to move around the city and visited the internment camp twice a week. He reported that George was in good health.

After VE Day, the end of the war in Europe, internees were in no doubt that it was only a matter of time before they would be liberated. Once Japan had surrendered, though, they were unsure how its soldiers would react in the period between the dropping of the atom bomb and the arrival of Allied troops. They remained in the camp and kept a low profile. The only celebration was a game of cricket. As the hidden underground army began to surface, Brigadier Victor Jacques, SOE's representative in Bangkok, visited the camp in uniform and made an eloquent speech that told them nothing.

George Windred was liberated from the internment camp on 3rd September 1945, by this time seriously ill with malaria and dysentery. Coincidentally, he was flown to Singapore by a pilot who later became a colleague of George's son Richard Windred in the Mars foodstuffs group. He recovered in Singapore, where the drugs were available to treat him. After his return to the UK, he was able in November 1945, dressed in his uniform as a captain of the Intelligence Corps, to greet his son and wife as their ship arrived in Southampton from Australia.

The war had ended, and George Windred was very keen to continue in undercover work. In late November 1945, he was back in London, being interviewed by the head of his SOE department to determine his future. He was considered a good candidate for the organisation's Far East desk in London, a role he was willing to take on even though he preferred to work in the field. As SOE was just a few weeks from being closed down by Clement Attlee's Labour Government, it is not entirely clear which organisation was in prospect. SOE's post-war role had been the subject of considerable controversy since mid-1944.

George appears to have worked for a time on the China desk of the Foreign Office but then joined ICI on technical service for the insecticide Gammaxene. He travelled extensively to Brazil in the late 1940s, working on the fight against Chagas disease. Whether he was able also to continue to serve Britain in some other way, of which we are not aware, is open to speculation.

George died in 1964 in Surrey. Gwen survived him by fifteen years; Richard became a senior executive with the Mars food group. George Loftus Windred was a tough Australian officer of Britain's Intelligence Corps and an unacknowledged fighter in a global war.

CHAPTER 4

Securing SOE

*'If you have built castles in the air, your work need not be lost; that
is where they should be. Now put the foundations under them.'*
Henry David Thoreau, *Walden*

Make Safe

THE IMPRESSION ONE GAINS OF SOE is a pervasive sense of
independence and buccaneering spirit. The problem of instilling a
sense of security into this group of loners was one of SOE's greatest
challenges, on a par with defending its existence against its many
Whitehall enemies.

Yet the countless stories of missions behind enemy lines confirm
the importance of security. Chance can play an important role; many
tragic cases have been recounted of agents captured, tortured and
executed because of an unlucky encounter with a police spot check or
betrayal by an informer. But it does seem that many of those who
survived – Francis Cammaerts or Tony Brooks of French Section, for
example – did so because of their obsessive concern for security. To
make this a matter of routine required patience, meticulous attention
to detail and a healthy dose of suspicion. This was the frame of mind
that the instructors at Beaulieu, the Field Security NCOs and the
officers of the Security Section tried to instil in the trainee agents.
Not all were receptive.

Beefing up the Security Section

The need to keep SOE secure was recognised early. Few useful
precedents existed, though, so the Security Section's tasks developed
in an *ad hoc* way. Just as for other aspects of SOE – operational

planning, intelligence, radio communications – it was only in mid-1941 that the roles and therefore the security needs of the organisation had crystallised sufficiently to enable a properly structured response.

The Security Section was SOE's point of contact with MI5, SIS and New Scotland Yard. This liaison was particularly important in the early days, so that SOE could add to its understanding of how to 'do' irregular warfare, by learning from those who had experience of fighting against the Irish Republican Army and the like. More obvious reasons for liaising with the other agencies were, for instance, to find likely candidates for agent duties from among individuals registered as 'aliens' and to work together on identifying security risks to the rapidly increasing network of training establishments.

The reorganisation and expansion of the Section in July 1941, to reflect the growing security needs, positioned it as part of a new Intelligence and Security Directorate under the highly experienced, respected and charming Air Commodore Archie Boyle. Boyle's avuncular nature was deceptive; he was knowledgeable and discerning. Responsible for security under Boyle was Major-General John Lakin, ex-Indian Army and ex-MI5, whose failing health led eventually to a transfer to a less demanding position supervising security in Scotland. He died in post there.

In its new form, the Section divided responsibilities into 'general' and 'operational' security. General security included the whole range of routine measures that any secret organisation might need, but the 'upstart' SOE also needed to convince outsiders like MI5 that its security was up to scratch. To find personnel for these purposes, SOE often turned pragmatically to an in-house source of high-quality men trained in intelligence and security: the Field Security Sections. An example is Norman Mott, a member of 64 FSS who was promoted into the Security Section and took responsibility for the SOE buildings and training schools in and near London, together with travel control. Arthur Baird, a member of 63 Section, was commissioned as Jack O'Reilly's deputy for liaison with the police, with HM Customs and with other ministries. Others were engaged in vetting SOE personnel; up to 8,000 were vetted each year. As the Field Security Officers – Walmsley, Brown and Glanville-Brown – moved on, their places were filled by men promoted from the ranks of the Sections. William Martin, Anelyf Rees and C G 'Geoff' Holland were commissioned on various dates in the second half of 1941 to command 63, 64 and 65 Sections respectively. All went on to play significant roles elsewhere in SOE.

Holland worked on security at the 'Finishing Schools' at Beaulieu and then in Cairo and Italy as a major. Martin, a Scot, had been born in Petrograd, formerly and again today called St Petersburg, but the family returned to Britain when the Russian Revolution broke out in 1917. Fluent in French, he had grown up in Scotland and France, and had worked as a shipping clerk for the Cunard Line. After just over a year commanding 63 Section, he moved to Edinburgh and took responsibility for the Scottish security office. Late in 1944, he was transferred to India and was responsible for despatching agents of Force 136, SOE's clandestine operation in Japanese-occupied Southeast Asia.

Anelyf Rees came from relatively humble origins in the mining village of Trecynon in North Wales, son of a respected official in the local colliery. At the County School for boys in Aberdare, Anelyf showed himself to be intelligent and a fast learner. He won a coveted scholarship to the University College of Wales at Aberystwyth, where he learned something of military life in the university's Officer Training Corps and found time to gain a Double First-Class degree in History and Economics. The awards piled up. He was granted a further scholarship for postgraduate research and a Travelling Scholarship.

So the young Anelyf Rees, having already visited the Soviet Union at the age of 19, continued to travel widely. He studied from 1935 to 1937 at the *Institut Universitaire* in Geneva, researching into International Relations and gaining an MA with Distinction. He took full advantage of the money he had been awarded for travel, visiting France, Italy, Greece, Romania, Hungary, Austria and Germany in a Europe that was even then preparing for war. The contrast must have been extreme when he went for six months to the USA, where he lectured mostly at Carleton College in Northfield, Minnesota, but also gave lectures in Minneapolis, Chicago, Philadelphia, Washington DC and New York.

War was definitely visible on the horizon when Rees returned to Europe. He taught history in secondary schools in Wales, but spent his spare time working with refugees from Germany and Austria. During the Phoney War, Anelyf continued to teach, but matters became more urgent in mid-1940. After a spell in the Royal Engineers awaiting confirmation of his acceptance for Field Security, he turned up at the Intelligence Corps school at Winchester in October 1940. Given his fluent French and academic accomplishments, he was an obvious choice for SOE's Field Security Sections. The interview confirmed it.

As a mere lance-corporal in 64 Section, Anelyf Rees may have felt that his talents were not being recognised. A French-speaker, although unlike Teddy Bisset not of Anglo-French parentage, he found himself accompanying French agents through their preliminary training at Wanborough Manor and their paramilitary training in the Arisaig area. And of course Anelyf did everything the agents did: living off the land; stripping, reassembling and firing a variety of foreign weapons; working with explosives and demolitions; hand-to-hand combat taught by the legendary Bill Fairbairn and Eric Sykes. But the humble status did not last long. Anelyf Rees was quickly promoted into supervisory roles, as a sergeant, then as the company sergeant major, then in October 1941 – two days before his 29th birthday – commissioned as 64 Section's Field Security Officer. This gave him responsibility for security of the training at schools in southern England. He continued as a staff officer in the Security Section for the rest of the war, finishing as a captain in its Military Sub-Section.

However, the main reason the Field Security personnel had been recruited was to secure the operational side of SOE, and most of this work involved the agents under training in Britain.

Training for the Field

SOE is often known for its outrageous initiative and intrepid improvisation. But one thing quickly became clear in the early months of its existence: the key to successful support for resistance movements would be a well-trained body of agents. And if the organisation and the agents themselves were to survive, they would have to be both secured in their training and trained in security. By December 1940, plans were already in place for twenty training schools. With the help of the police, sites were identified that could be kept discreet and safe from curious outsiders. Often these were large houses and estates in remote areas. Not for nothing was SOE often known as 'Stately 'Omes of England'.

By early 1941, agent training had developed a structured pattern totalling about thirteen weeks, although the detail might vary for individuals with particular needs or existing skill sets. It generally started with a two- to three-week course of physical fitness training, fieldcraft, basic map-reading, Morse code and some work with weapons and explosives. Agents destined for the different country sections were trained at separate schools; Wanborough Manor, commanded by Coldstream Guards officer Major Roger de Wesselow, was the main preliminary assessment site for French Section.

The purpose of this first phase was as much selection as training. The personalities of the potential agents were closely observed: their courage, their resilience, their alcohol tolerance, their reticence or volubility, their reliability (important if they were to be entrusted with more cash or gold than they had ever seen in their lives). Up to half of them, judged for one reason or other to be unsuitable, returned to their former lives with only the vaguest idea of what they had been training for. From mid-1943, the preliminary schools were replaced by a much shorter 'Students Assessment Board' based on psychological appraisal, at Winterfold in Surrey.

Those who successfully completed the course at one of the preliminary schools or 'depots' moved on to paramilitary training at one of the 'Group A' schools in Inverness-shire, Scotland, centred on Arisaig House but based at up to nine separate houses. They were taught to strip, clean, reassemble and fire a whole range of weapons, by day and by night, in all kinds of weather. They mastered unarmed combat and silent killing, gaining the confidence to tackle any foe. They learned to navigate by day and night, to move undetected, to set ambushes, to control an armed group in a tactical situation, to blow up railway tracks. By the end of this phase of the training, they could be in little doubt about their future role.

Arisaig, Scotland

After parachute training, those who were selected to organise a Resistance 'circuit' or to be couriers went on to the Beaulieu 'Group B' Finishing Schools, which turned paramilitary trainees into secret agents. They remained segregated from other countries' students as they practised total immersion in their target language and learned how to recruit and lead a secure undercover network while staying out of enemy hands. Should they fail in this, they needed to know how to resist interrogation and, if they could escape, to survive on the run. Instructors with dubious backgrounds taught nefarious skills like lock-picking and safe-breaking. Out in the streets of towns and cities, students practised passing messages, moving around without being followed and tailing someone without being spotted. Those who were destined to become wireless operators or to carry out sabotage operations were sent to specialised training: normally at Thame Park in Oxfordshire for clandestine radio operation or at Brickendonbury Manor, near Hertford, for industrial sabotage.

SOE memorial Beaulieu

'Remember before God those men and women of the European Resistance Movement who were secretly trained at Beaulieu to fight their lonely battle against Hitler's Germany and who, before entering Nazi-occupied territory, here found some measure of the peace for which they fought.'

After specialist training or Beaulieu and the necessary operational briefings at a 'holding school', agents were ready for deployment. Most were not deployed immediately, though, and agents might have to wait, tense with anticipation, before the time came for their parachute drop, night landing into a tiny field or sea insertion. If they were made to wait too long without constructive operational training, they could easily stagnate.

All the phases of training took place in isolated locations under a mantle of secrecy. The Training Section in London designed and coordinated the various courses, but lacked influence in the SOE hierarchy over the relatively autonomous and secretive country sections. So did the Security Section, whose task was to ensure that the training stayed secret and to give the agents the best possible chance of survival in the field.

Fyffe of Inverlair

Lance-Corporal Aonghais Fyffe was sent by his Commanding Officer in April 1941 to meet Brigadier Gubbins at Fort William railway station. He had heard of Gubbins' exploits in the Norway campaign. He had also gained more knowledge of SOE than he should have, through hearing SOE staff officers chat to each other as he drove them from the railway station to Arisaig House and the other houses they were taking over for paramilitary training. 'They must have thought I had cloth ears heavily felted', he remarked, 'they just opened their mouths and let their tongues wag'.[27]

Aonghais Fyffe, 2002

---

[27] IWM Oral History 23100, Fyffe.

Fyffe was a feisty Scot who joined SOE early, but not via 63, 64 or 65 Sections. He had received intelligence training in 1940 at Winchester and Matlock and was posted as a lance-corporal to No 49 FSS in Fort William, responsible for the security of No 1 Protected Area. This was a vast area of remote northwest Scotland, guarded and permit-controlled, in which the Independent Companies trained. Hailing from Dundee and married to a girl who had grown up a few miles from Fort William, Fyffe knew the area intimately. More to the point, he and his family were themselves well known and trusted in the Highlands.

He collected Gubbins from the front carriage of the 2.10 West Highland train and was subjected to a stream of questions about his time at the University of St Andrews and other aspects of his personal life. Gubbins was shocked at how much Fyffe knew about the 'Inter-Services Research Bureau' and its activities in Scotland, but Fyffe's explanation – overheard conversations, monitored phone calls, censored correspondence – seemed to encourage him. He announced that Fyffe would be commissioned as from that day and was to report to Baker Street in three weeks.

Fyffe's first job as an officer was at Thame Park in Oxfordshire, then being used as the Spanish Country Section's holding school. There he found himself responsible for security and intelligence, as well as helping to oversee the training of a bunch of battle-seasoned Spanish Communists who had fought and been defeated in the Spanish Civil War. They had escaped into France and had been accepted there, provided they joined the French Foreign Legion.

Many had served France well in Africa and in defending her against the German *Blitzkrieg*. Just before the fall of France, they embarked on a British vessel in Bordeaux and landed in Britain, where they enrolled in the Pioneer Corps, the supposedly non-combatant service organisation where foreign nationals could help the war effort.

SOE had taken over the Thame Park group and was maintaining their fitness and fighting skills through 20-mile route marches and night navigation exercises, with a view to using them in Spain if the need or opportunity arose: if for instance the Germans pressed on from France into Spain. Any SOE operations in neutral countries were a sensitive subject, though; the Foreign Office looked on them cautiously and imposed constraints.

The Spanish troops were allowed outside the estate for relaxation in the evenings, under the cover of being Mexican volunteers in the Allied cause. They were tough, and it was a brave local man or off-duty soldier who picked a fight. Nevertheless, Fyffe maintained good relations with the local police. He and his colleagues made a habit of going out after dinner, very visibly calling in at local pubs and dance halls. Trouble was rare.

Aonghais Fyffe stayed only five months with the Spaniards, during which time they were not given any operational missions. In September 1941, during a weekend leave in London with his wife, who was visiting from Scotland, he was urgently sought out by Baker Street. He had to collect his kit from Thame Park, see his wife on to a train to Scotland and then travel with Whetmore on a different train to take over the newly formed 'Cooler'.

This was a new concept, and unusual in that it brought different nationalities together under one roof. But it was necessary, because the trainers had a problem. Some individuals might not reach the high physical and mental standards of the paramilitary course in the Highlands and some – now better informed – might also decide that they were not suited for this new life as an agent in enemy territory. What could be done with those who could not progress further with the training? They knew too much.

The solution was to create a special kind of school at Inverlair Lodge in remote Scotland. Officially 'No 6 Special Workshop School', Inverlair was known as 'The Cooler'. Those who did not successfully complete training could not be let loose with the secrets they had learned. But Inverlair was not a prison. Aonghais Fyffe and his staff kept the men gainfully employed, but isolated from the outside world, until it was deemed safe to send them back to their units. Agents or members of country sections who were found to be unreliable, but not warranting a court martial, were sent to the Cooler for six months or so before being sent back to their units or into civilian life. The first of them were Italians who had seemed to be promising anti-Fascists at first but turned out variously to be too unfit, too talkative or too unstable, or whose motivation was too shaky. Indeed, the problem of what to do with these men had led to the decision to open the Cooler. But soon Belgians, Spaniards and others arrived. Over the four years of its existence, eighty-one men were required to 'live in retirement' at Inverlair, of whom two were held on behalf of SIS.

Aonghais Fyffe was remarkably successful in keeping the atmosphere at the Cooler disciplined and busy, but relatively relaxed. He remained Commandant of Inverlair until it was preparing for closure in early 1944, but from 1943 he had broader responsibilities for the security of all of the secret training schools in Scotland. His schedule of weekly travel across Scotland was gruelling.

By early 1944, the Cooler was no longer needed and it was run down. Fyffe joined the Security Section in London in February as Head of the Military Sub-Section, with responsibility for all SOE training schools.

Keeping it Secure

Ensuring the security of the training schools was a task to be done both inside and outside the barbed wire. In its most straightforward form, this was not much different from Field Security for an Army formation. Gilbert Smith, a member of 64 Section who had shared a 'billet' with Teddy Bisset when they first joined SOE, specialised in local security at training schools and the other SOE 'stations' dotted around the country.

Gilbert hailed from Cheshire and had studied French at the University of Liverpool, with a year abroad at Caen. He became a schoolmaster and in December 1937 found himself teaching English in Berlin, rather like John Le Carré's fictional character George Smiley. Smiley was there to recruit agents among the young people with whom he came in contact. No evidence exists that Smith had any such role, but it is intriguing that he chose Germany rather than

France for his teaching job in a period of increasing international tension. By the late 1930s, the SIS network of 'Passport Control Officers' attached to British embassies was thoroughly compromised. Claude Dansey, the devious deputy head of SIS, had set up his own parallel 'Z' network of amateur agents.

After spending the summer of 1938 back in Britain, Gilbert Smith returned to Berlin to teach English in a secondary school, while studying German language and culture at Berlin University, today's Humboldt University. Berlin in 1938 had an edgy atmosphere. The streets were full of military personnel in uniform. Security was tight. Change was in the air, and not in a positive sense.

The Nazi Party had consolidated its grip on German society, including the education system, and Germany was increasing its military pressure abroad. Few 'un-German' books remained to be burned. In January 1939, Hitler threatened the annihilation of the Jewish race in Europe;[28] by the summer, all Jewish businesses had been closed.

Gilbert left Germany in July 1939, taught in English schools for a while, was called up into the Intelligence Corps in July 1940 and joined SOE as a member of 64 FSS in February 1941. He first fulfilled his security role at the Camberley Reception Depot, a storage facility in Surrey from which equipment for SOE stations in the UK was distributed to wherever it was needed.

Smith moved after three months to Fawley Court, a neo-classical country house designed by Sir Christopher Wren, with gardens by Capability Brown flanking the River Thames. The house, near Henley in Oxfordshire, was the inspiration for Toad Hall in *The Wind in the Willows*. For SOE, it was a training school for wireless operators. Smith stayed in touch with the local police, visited cafes and pubs like the *Old Bell* or the *Bird in Hand*, investigated reports of insecurity and monitored what local people thought was going on at the school.

---

[28] Speech to the Reichstag, 30th January 1939.

Fawley Court

Gilbert Smith spent a couple of months on similar duties at Audley End in Essex, the holding school where Polish agents received final training and briefing, before moving away from the training environment to ensure local security at a secret location in Hertfordshire. He was tasked with ensuring that the population in the nearby villages, and others further afield, did not get an inkling of what was going on at a former private hotel just outside the village of Welwyn. Taken over as a headquarters and a radio communications centre by SIS's Section D before the outbreak of war and absorbed with Section D into SOE, 'The Frythe' became Station IX, SOE's main technical research centre. Here, in temporary huts in the extensive grounds, ingenious engineers and technicians developed specialist weapons, explosives and camouflage devices for SOE and other parts of the armed forces.

Many of Station IX's inventions had the first three letters of the location, Welwyn, in their names; the *Welbike* was a tiny lightweight parachutable motorcycle, the *Welman* a one-man midget submarine, the *Welmine* a floating motorised explosive charge. Many of the devices developed by SOE went on to be used by other units, such as Commando forces and the Special Air Service. One of SOE's several cover names, the Inter-Service Research Bureau, was later used primarily for the technical branch of the organisation. Gilbert Smith's task was to ensure that these secrets were kept secret.

Welbike in parachute container

Smith moved on. For several months from November 1942, he was assigned to liaison with MI5 at the interrogation centre described later in this chapter. Then, in July 1943, he was commissioned into the Security Branch and took over Travel Control as a lieutenant. Suffering from poor health, he did not serve abroad, even after the D-Day invasion of the Continent. An opportunity for greater use of his proficiency in German arose in September 1944, though, when he was transferred to the German Section to work at Special Training School 2.

Bellasis House, on Box Hill near Dorking, had been a training school and holding depot for a variety of nationalities, including the Czech SOE agents who assassinated Reinhardt Heydrich in Prague in 1942. Now, though, it served as a school that trained German prisoners-of-war with anti-Nazi sympathies to return to their homeland as SOE agents. These were the '*Bonzos*', of whom more later. Gilbert served as an interrogation and security officer at STS 2 and was very effective in the role, but ill health caused a move to the Section's headquarters in London. There he prepared and mounted operations on Germany for others to implement.

Keeping Company

Back to those agents under training.

Every cohort of trainees had one or more Field Security NCOs accompanying them through each phase of their training, with language skills appropriate to the target country. As Anelyf Rees put it in his 1944 report on SOE's Field Security personnel, these NCOs had been plucked out of Intelligence Corps training, hand-picked not just for their knowledge of the particular languages and countries, but also for their 'natural faculty for assessing another man's character correctly, quickly and without prejudice'.[29] As far as possible, the NCOs participated in every aspect of the training, working alongside the students inside and outside the classroom. They tried to be helpful and encouraging, assisting with language difficulties and personal issues. Even so, their primary purpose could not be hidden. Students, and the country sections to which they belonged, often resented the intrusion. Trainees compared Field Security to the Gestapo. A negative attitude to their security 'advisors' cost some of them dear when they encountered the real Gestapo.

---

[29] TNA HS 7/31, D/CE.M.1 (Anelyf Rees) to AD/P, (Archie Boyle), 3rd October 1944, Report on FSP Activity, p.6.

At the preliminary schools, the Field Security NCOs were looking out for a trainee's general suitability for work as an agent. Some trainees, like Teddy Bisset's 'sleep-talker' at Wanborough Manor, might be considered for exclusion without them knowing it. Some became garrulous when they had too much to drink; to test for this, alcohol was made freely available. Others proved unable to withstand the relentless physical exercise. All of this was reported to Peter Lee in the NCOs' weekly reports on their charges.

The more challenging paramilitary training in northern Scotland brought less obvious issues to the surface, in those who had survived the preliminary training. Corporal Arthur Ronnfeldt, who had joined SOE as a Field Security NCO in October 1942, reported on a potential Dutch agent that he was 'inclined to be rather noisy when he first arrived', had 'confidence in his own abilities', perhaps 'greatly strengthened by his former experiences as a Dutch mounted policeman, after the occupation of his country', when he had 'found it very easy to hoodwink the Boche'. He was also 'very fond of the society of women' and sometimes 'a little unsteady on his feet when returning home'. 'He may have to be watched for over-confidence', was Ronnfeldt's judgment, although after the man's engagement to a female agent he seemed 'to have become a reformed character'.[30] His confidence may have been dented when he was found to have a severe fear of heights and had to be helped down from the high-level training apparatus. When he got to the parachute training school at Ringway – like many with vertigo – he found travelling in an aircraft, and even jumping from it, less of a problem.

The Field Security NCOs were not expected to take an interest in the backgrounds of the trainees, their political leanings or the nature and location of the operation for which they were training. But they did try to discern the motivation of those they were accompanying. Were they driven primarily by a love of their country? Could they be trusted with large sums of money and – more importantly – with the

---

[30] TNA HS 9/114/1.

lives of others? Did they have too romantic a sense of the 'adventure' they were about to undertake? Did they recognise the risks?

The NCOs were not there just to assess trainees. They also gave lectures on security and tried by any means possible to convince the students of the importance of personal security to their future survival. By the time the students moved on to the Group B schools at Beaulieu, the presence of the accompanying Field Security NCOs was largely unnecessary. The students who had survived the earlier training had proved themselves. They also had a very clear understanding of what they were letting themselves in for. Trainee agents were taught about the different enemy counter-intelligence services and the police forces of occupied countries. They learned how to concoct cover stories, how to blend in and not appear conspicuous, how to maintain constant vigilance and plan for unexpected emergencies.

The skills were practised in 'real' situations, in British towns among local people unaware of what was going on in their midst. Field Security NCOs would play the part of clandestine contacts or observe the trainees' behaviour. The Security Section had also secretly employed Christine Chilver, an intelligent, astute and attractive 22-year-old *agente provocatrice,* cover name *Fifi.* Posing as a French journalist, she would strike up a conversation with the trainee agent in a hotel bar, establish a relationship and report back on how much she had been able to learn about his or her real identity.[31]

Sergeant Robert Stebbing-Allen, an SOE Field Security NCO from December 1941 who had been a lawyer in Haslemere, Surrey, before the war, reported on a two-day exercise in the Midland town of Loughborough. The agent was 'painstaking and intelligent' and did 'remarkable work' following suspects, meeting agents in cafes, passing messages in person or through dead letter boxes, developing a cover story and resisting interrogation. He was discreet, his manner was natural and his cover convincing.[32] Whether such an exemplary

---

[31] TNA HS 9/307/3
[32] TNA HS 9/166/7

performance in the artificial training situation can be sustained in the field is a different question. Reports suggest that the same agent's activities in France were less than secure. Let it suffice here to say that personal attitudes are as important as security 'techniques'. No amount of training can help an agent who is not convinced of its importance to his or her survival.

The often-contentious relationship between the Security Section and the various country sections was paralleled in each agent's mindset and behaviour. It was difficult for an agent to strike the right balance between security and effective action. M R D Foot quotes one SOE operative's principle: 'Caution axiomatic, but over-caution results in nothing done'. 'Those who bothered incessantly about security survived', suggests Foot, 'but few of them had much beyond survival to their credit. To strike and then to survive is the real test'.[33] Few achieved this balance.

Interrogation

In late 1941, an interrogation sub-section was formed within the Security Section, consisting of one Field Security Officer, Lieutenant McMillan, and two Field Security NCOs, Frank Pickering of 64 Section and Albert Vennix, who had joined SOE in July 1941. By agreement with MI5 and SIS, their task was to interrogate newly arrived non-British individuals, or 'aliens', at the Royal Victoria Patriotic Schools in Wandsworth, southwest London. The RVPS had been built in 1859 to house girls orphaned by the Crimean War. In the Second World War it became MI5's 'London Reception Centre', where those arriving in the UK from overseas were carefully vetted and interrogated before being set free, interned or – if found to be German agents – offered an 'opportunity' to become double agents. The alternative was bleak.

The SOE interrogators at RVPS extracted and collated intelligence of special interest to the organisation, through interrogations in

---

[33] *SOE: an outline history of the Special Operations Executive 1940-1946*, M R D Foot, 2008, p. 173.

French, German, Spanish, Flemish and Dutch. Also, they looked out for men and women who might respond well to SOE training, passing details to country sections. However, the process was not successful. The sub-section was disbanded in mid-1942 and Captain Richard Warden was tasked to liaise with MI5, whose RVPS interrogation reports he circulated to the relevant country sections.

Design for Royal Victoria Patriotic Asylum, 1857

Dick Warden was a well-travelled Old Harrovian, amateur steeplechase rider and racehorse trainer who had studied at Cornell University. He joined SOE on 14th January 1941 as a member of 63 FSS, working as a lance-corporal on the security of the Group B training schools at Beaulieu. He also dealt with security for operations into Norway from the Shetlands and into France by the Small-Scale Raiding Force. Within a few months, though, he was selected for commissioning into the Security Branch. Alert, sophisticated and trustworthy, he soon became the linchpin of the relationship between SOE and MI5.

The reduced liaison arrangement seemed for a while to fit the bill, but it became clear during 1942 that it was far from sensible to leave security in the field to the country sections. German counter-intelligence officers were ingenious in their attempts to penetrate SOE networks. Although the true extent of their success was not yet known, by the start of 1943 it was clear that there was a serious problem. MI5 insisted that all returning agents who had been in contact with the enemy must be assumed compromised unless proved otherwise. Escapes could of course be faked.

The system was tightened up. Until then, deployed SOE agents, like those of SIS, had been exempt from 'travel control' on their return. From January 1943, country sections were required to give details of all returning agents to the Security Directorate. A 'Special Security Section' had been set up at Bayswater under Dick Warden, and later under Aonghais Fyffe, to interrogate agents, to test the personal security of the agent, to assess whether his or her in-country circuits had been penetrated and to glean any useful intelligence that could be passed to the country sections or to the technical, supply and camouflage sections. Every scrap of information about travel passes, identity cards, clothing and daily routine in enemy territory could be useful. The agent would write a report on the mission – some country sections were very slow in passing it on to Warden – from which the interrogator would question him or her on doubtful or unclear points.

Later, the Bayswater Section's role was expanded to include investigating all allegations of enemy penetration or double agents associated with SOE. This still fell short of responsibility for all aspects of operational security, which remained with the country sections. Information gleaned in interrogations was followed up with country sections, normally with the help of MI5, to seek out clarity in what was often a quagmire of doubt and obscurity. One agent might accuse another of treachery, but both of their stories might be convincing, with corroboration by a third party unavailable.

In two cases Warden was able to prove that agents had been 'turned' and sent back to penetrate SOE in Britain. In a third case, the accusation could not be proved true or false, so the individual was removed from operations. In yet other cases, Warden judged that the agent's security was so far compromised, perhaps innocently, that he or she could not be sent back to the field.

Clues that a Resistance circuit was being controlled by the enemy, or that an individual had been 'turned', were often inconclusive. MI5, often with justification, tended to see the security of country sections as lax and to favour suspicion and caution over operational needs. Country sections defended their agents, whom they thought they knew intimately, against allegations they saw as unsubstantiated. They were reluctant to allow security doubts to interfere with their ongoing operations. The Security Section tried to take the middle ground. But where penetration had taken place, the unwelcome facts were only slowly accepted.

Penetration

One of the greatest controversies about SOE has raged over the subsequent decades: to what extent was the organisation penetrated by the enemy?

It was certainly 'penetrated' by an ally. Apart from Kim Philby, who soon left for SIS, there were several Communist sympathisers among the organisation's ranks. James Klugmann in Cairo and John Eyre of the Albanian Section in Bari were among them. The Soviet Union was a valued and essential ally. Nevertheless, the SOE staff were not naive; Gubbins, for one, was highly suspicious of the Soviet regime. When Ormond Uren, a staff member in the Hungarian Section, was found to have passed details of SOE's organisation to the Soviet Embassy, he was tried *in camera* and sentenced to seven years' imprisonment.

The idea that SOE was a left-wing organisation could derive from the party affiliation of Hugh Dalton, the minister, and provide ammunition for competitors in Whitehall. Harry Rée, who had been a conscientious objector to the war for political reasons, thought the idea laughable: the top people all came from private banking in the City, he suggested.

Security precautions in the SOE headquarters and stations were tight. They were founded on the assumption that enemy agents might be watching SOE in Baker Street and elsewhere. SOE staff were not to recognise each other in the street or to admit that they were part of a secret organisation. Country sections kept themselves to themselves. In theory, agents knew each other only by their training alias. Before the war ended, it became almost certain that all German spies arriving in Britain had been imprisoned, executed or persuaded to act as double agents. Before becoming SOE's Director of Intelligence and Security, Archie Boyle had been instrumental in defining how widely knowledge of this highly successful 'double-cross' system should be shared. The espionage threat in Britain was minimal.

Not so in the field. Soon after the war ended, SOE was able to put together reports by returning agents, information from locally recruited members of SOE circuits and interrogation of German counter-intelligence officers and their collaborators, to assemble a clearer picture of how successful penetration had been.

Agents might be detected by snap checks and road blocks, often carried out by local police or militia who were more likely to spot forged identity documents than were German soldiers. A person found to be carrying a large sum of money, weapons or explosives would immediately be arrested. The wireless operator's radio set weighed 30 pounds or more and was almost impossible to hide.

More deliberate and long-term methods of capturing agents were the use of direction-finding equipment to detect illegal transmitters and the employment of collaborators as '*Vertrauensmänner*', or '*V-Männer*' (trusted local agents), acting as informers or *agents provocateurs*. Without their help, the Germans would have been unable to unearth agent circuits. Plenty of local people were willing to help in this way, perhaps through anonymous denunciation but often in return for substantial payment. Orchestrating these different tools could pay big dividends.

Once an agent was captured, he or she was meant to remain silent, especially for the first forty-eight hours after capture. These principles were drummed into agents in training, but captors could use many techniques and tricks. The Field Security men's training could only go so far and could quickly be forgotten under pressure.

Country section staff officers were often over-optimistic about their agents' ability to withstand torture or more subtle persuasion.

The classic example of how to conduct successful counter-intelligence and, on the other hand, how not to run agents in the field was the famous and still controversial '*Englandspiel*' (England game) run by the Netherlands branches of Heinrich Himmler's *Sicherheitsdienst* of the Nazi Party and the *Abwehr*, the German military intelligence service. Progress against Allied subversion was often hampered by rivalry between the two organisations, but the German counter-intelligence operation was nevertheless impressively efficient.

Abwehr officer Hermann Giskes, who wrote after the war about his counter-intelligence success, knew it as *Unternehmen Nordpol* (*Operation North Pole*). Through capturing a Dutch SIS agent in 1941 with copies of previous messages on his person, the Germans were able to make a start in deciphering SIS codes, which SOE was also using at the time. The capture of two further SIS agents in early 1942 helped to consolidate this process. A Dutch *V-Mann* was able to insinuate his way into the SOE sabotage team sent, as part of the 'Plan for Holland' agreed between SOE and the Dutch government in exile, to train and equip a Secret Army in the Netherlands. He fed false intelligence to the agents.

When wireless operator Huub Lauwers was arrested on 6th March 1942, he had not had time to dispose of three enciphered messages he had been about to send. He was amazed to watch the Germans decipher one of them, helped by their prior knowledge of the codes and the fact that they had provided some of the content. He agreed to send the messages, but did not include the necessary security checks. The Dutch Section in London ignored the 'error' on this and several more occasions. When he inserted 'CAU' and 'GHT' in the jumbled preamble of a message, the message was 'topped and tailed' by the wireless operators before being sent to the staff officers. His warning did not get through.

More agents were dropped, only to be arrested on landing. The Germans were able to surprise each of them by the depth of their knowledge and to point out the futility of keeping silent. Every additional captured agent helped Giskes to build up that knowledge. There must be a traitor in London, they thought. Giskes used the captured radio sets to play back radio traffic to London, requesting arms, equipment and more agents to be sent. They were, and the number of sets under German control eventually reached double figures. Two were operated by SOE agents under duress, the remainder by Germans.

Suspicions arose in London from mid-1943 and SOE's Security Section tried to work out which radio transmitters were under German control. Dick Warden liaised with MI5 and SIS to get to the bottom of the question. But the Dutch Section – in part to investigate the security situation – continued to drop agents, explosives and arms in Holland, into the hands of the waiting Germans.

Only in November 1943 did a message come through from two agents, code-named *Chive* and *Sprout*, who had managed to reach the Dutch Legation in Switzerland after escaping from the concentration camp where the captured agents were being held. The two warned that the entire SOE network in Holland was under German control. By the time they reached London after a slow and arduous journey through Spain, Giskes had used one of the captured sets to tell SOE that the pair had gone over to the Gestapo. Also, the stories they told interrogators in Spain and after they reached London were inconsistent. Suspected of having faked their escape, they were incarcerated until after D-Day and only later vindicated.

SOE maintained routine radio contact with the blown sets, in the hope that this might help to keep the captives alive. In the long run, it did not help. Most of the more than fifty captured agents were shot before the end of the war. Giskes, realising that further subterfuge was pointless, sent a sardonic message on 1st April 1944 to the Dutch Section leaders by name, thanking them for their cooperation.

The over-optimistic view of the Dutch Section about their agents, the lack of a healthy suspicion and respect for security procedures, the exclusion of the Security Section from routine radio security matters, the unwillingness of SIS to cooperate with the upstart SOE in the investigation and, perhaps, SOE's fears for its existence in the face of external hostility in Whitehall: all of these factors led to a disaster. When transmissions from agents' radios lacked the expected security checks, nobody seems to have thought of putting trick questions into the responses, to establish whether it was a genuine oversight or something more sinister. Dozens of highly trained agents were dropped directly into captivity, many of them to their eventual death. Tons of arms and equipment were 'donated' to the enemy. Agent by agent, the Germans were able to gain control of the Dutch circuits and maintain it for over a year. The 'Plan for Holland' was set at naught.

Englandspiel plaque, Den Haag

The Dutch Section and the government-in-exile were able very quickly to put new agents into the field in support of Resistance groups but independent of the blown networks. But the damage was done; the invading Allied armies were instructed to have nothing to do with the Dutch underground.

A small mistake could have devastating results, not just for the individual concerned but for hundreds of others. Conspiracy theories have been propounded as to the 'real' reason the Dutch Section continued to send agents. The story shows that it may be easier to capture agents than to be one, and has to be seen in the context of

MI5's total success in running over 100 German double agents in Britain.

Holland was not the only place where penetration of SOE circuits was successful. It also happened in Norway and in Belgium. And in France.

CHAPTER 5

Into the Field

*'Any nation that uses [partisan warfare] intelligently will, as a
rule, gain some superiority over those who disdain its use.'*
Carl von Clausewitz, *On War*

Agent Valentin

AGENT VALENTIN PARACHUTED FROM A HALIFAX BOMBER into
a moonlit night sky in the early hours of 16th June 1943 and landed
near Châtillon-sur-Cher, in the valley of the River Cher close to
Valençay and about 170 kilometres southwest of Paris. With
Bertrand, the circuit organiser for whom he was to be wireless
operator, he was to take over part of the extensive Paris-based
Prosper circuit operating in the Ardennes region near the Belgian
border. The independent circuit was to be known as *Archdeacon*.

The *parachutage* was met by Resistance leader Roger Couffrant
and a reception party. It went smoothly, and *Valentin* and *Bertrand*
spent the next few days in hiding on an isolated estate, as their new
Resistance friends received supply drops and worked on improving
the newcomers' false papers. On 19th June, the pair were collected by
Resistance agent Pierre Culioli and SOE operative Yvonne Rudellat –
who worked together on sabotage and drop zone selection under
cover as a married couple – to stay for a further night at *Le Cercle*, a
forester's cottage near Veilleins.

Meanwhile, a security operation involving several thousand
German troops had descended on the area, looking for parachutists.
Acting on intelligence, the *Sicherheitsdienst* had decided to close in on

the Resistance circuits it had been monitoring. During the night of Sunday 20th June, Couffrant and a group of *résistants* moving arms and explosives from a parachute drop to a safe hiding place were stopped at a checkpoint and arrested. Early on Monday morning, not knowing of the arrests, Culioli and Rudellat collected agents *Bertrand* and *Valentin* from *Le Cercle* and set off in a Citroën car to a local station to catch the train to Paris. They did not get far.

Le Cercle, Veilleins, one of the safe houses where the two agents were hidden

In the village of Dhuizon, where Couffrant had been captured, German soldiers stopped the car. They sent agents *Bertrand* and *Valentin* to the *Mairie* – the village hall – to join the crowd of villagers whose papers were being checked. Culioli and Rudellat were forced to drive there, but their papers were in order and they returned to the Citroën. They sat in the car near the *Mairie* with the engine running, unable to help the two agents being questioned inside. When a German soldier came out and called them back into the building, they realised they could do nothing more. Culioli sped away, heading west, chased by three cars filled with German soldiers. The fugitives made it through the next village but soon thereafter came to another checkpoint and road-block near Bracieux. Yvonne was shot in the neck by a German guard and collapsed, apparently dead. To avoid being captured alive, Pierre tried to drive the Citroën into a wall, but it ended up in a garden. He was brought back to join *Bertrand* and *Valentin* in captivity at Dhuizon.

The two parachuted agents had had little chance to survive the document check. Neither had native-standard French; *Valentin*'s had been called 'villainous' by an SOE staff officer. A carefully concocted cover story – being from Belgium or Brittany – might get them through a cursory check by a German soldier, but would not fool a real interrogator.

The money belt around *Bertrand*'s waist, containing a large quantity of French currency obtained from a bank in London but issued before the war, would soon be discovered. And the parcel 'hidden in plain sight' in the car but disguised by being addressed to a French prisoner-of-war in Germany, would quickly be opened. It contained letters, written in unencoded English from French Section in London to SOE agents in France, and new crystals for the radio transmitters.

All three men were arrested and hauled away to prison. Yvonne Rudellat, who had been thought dead, in fact survived and was taken to hospital under German guard. From arriving by parachute, *Bertrand* and *Valentin* lasted less than a week in France before they were captured.

The Canadian Agent

Valentin's false French papers claimed that his name was Jean Charles Maulnier. His operational name in England had been *Plumber*. In reality, he was a Canadian called John Kenneth Macalister. *Bertrand* was Canadian too; he was an officer of the Canadian Intelligence Corps named Frank Pickersgill, but unlike *Valentin* he had not been a member of the Field Security Sections that are the primary concern of this book.

Ken Macalister was born in the early months of the First World War, in the town of Guelph, Ontario, often known as the Royal City. His father was a newspaperman of Scottish extraction, his mother a Roman Catholic who traced her roots back to Ireland.

Ken Macalister

Ken was a highly intelligent young man with an independent mind. After studying law for four years with distinction at the University of Toronto, he was accepted as one of two successful candidates from Ontario for the prestigious Rhodes Scholarship at the University of Oxford, which included a stipend for living expenses and travel. In October 1937, he arrived for the start of the Michaelmas Term at the misleadingly named New College; it had been founded in 1379 by William of Wykeham.

After his first year at Oxford, Ken spent the Long Vacation in the home of a French professor, to improve the standard of the French he had learned in Canada. He became more and more interested in French culture and law. Reluctantly at first, the Trustees of the Rhodes Trust eventually agreed to his unusual request that he spend his third year studying at the *Université de Paris*, otherwise known as the Sorbonne. He would be required to return to Oxford if the situation in France became unsafe. It did.

Despite the advice of his supervisor at the Rhodes Trust in Oxford, Ken seemed determined to stay in France after war broke out in September 1939. He transferred in November 1939 to the University of Caen in Normandy and came up with endless logistical and administrative reasons why it would be difficult to return to England. The real reason was more straightforward. He had begun a relationship with Jeannine, the 19-year-old daughter of the French professor who had invited him as a house guest. They had married in October 1939, she was pregnant and the fact that the Rhodes Scholarship was only open to single men was an unfortunate complication.

By the time he came clean to his supervisor, Ken had returned to Oxford, leaving his new wife in France, and surprised his tutor by achieving the best results of his class in his final examinations. Despite his deceit, the Rhodes Trustees treated him leniently.

While in France, Ken had applied to the French Army, but his poor eyesight had disqualified him. Back in England with his Oxford degree successfully completed, he felt even more convinced that he should contribute to the war effort. Many students had interrupted their studies to join the armed forces. He applied to several units, but his eyesight was always the obstacle.

Finally, one opening presented itself. He was accepted in July 1940 to join what was then, if only for a little longer, called the Field Security Police. As he waited for his call-up letter, emotional pressure from his mother increased, to ease her worries and come home to his family in Canada.

There was also the unexpected pull of academic ambition; Ken was invited to take up a lectureship at the University of Toronto. He vacillated, but with encouragement from his Oxford supervisor and some reassurance from his parents, he eventually stuck to his commitment to the Army. In September 1940, he became a rather unsettled trainee at the requisitioned King Alfred's College in Winchester, the Field Security Depot for the Intelligence Corps. He was under the less than tender ministrations of long-serving Guards NCOs determined to whip the motley collection of flabby intellectuals into shape. The highly-strung Ken was perhaps more susceptible than most to the pressures of the basic training, but he was not the only one to hate it. Nevertheless, separation from his young wife back in occupied France and lack of news about their unborn child increased his stress. He later learned that their daughter had been born in September 1940 but died soon afterwards.

When the fledgling SOE came looking for suitable talent at Winchester for its new Field Security Sections, Ken Macalister was an obvious choice. His proven intelligence and knowledge of French were obvious assets. On 1st February 1941, he became a 'founder member' of the second Field Security Section to be formed, No 64, at Guildford, with Teddy Bisset as one his eleven comrades and a billet with a local family.

Ken did well in his new tasks, participating in the twelve-week cycle of paramilitary, parachute and explosives training with groups of potential agents for French Section, and making weekly reports on them to Peter Lee. When periods of leave came, he was of course unable to be reunited with Jeannine in Normandy. He spent the time with the family of Eric and Harry Rée, brothers who served in SOE and who appear later in this chapter.

Ken made no secret of his desire to be awarded a commission. Perhaps his awareness that Jeannine was short of money gave him a financial incentive for promotion from the lowly rank of lance-corporal. The SOE hierarchy certainly thought him worthy of a commission, although perhaps in an office environment rather than in an operational role. In June 1941, he was sent on a special course of instruction that would normally have resulted in a commission, but the associated project fell through.

He came back to Field Security, joining 65 Section as a sergeant, and worked alongside his friend Harry Rée on the security of wireless operators under training at Thame Park in Oxfordshire. This entailed much more than checking that doors were locked and searching offices for unsecured classified documents. Towards the end of the agents' training, Harry and Ken installed the trainees in safe houses (usually courtesy of members of Harry's large family) for a week at a time and helped them to develop their sense of security: transmitting coded messages to them as their controllers, arranging a rendezvous in a public place or rousting them out of bed in the guise of Gestapo officers to question them and see how well they had hidden their bulky radio sets.

Like Harry Rée, though, Ken was keen to move from security to a more active operational role in France. They both pestered Peter Lee to allow them to do so, but he understandably vetoed the move. Both men knew almost everything there was to be known about SOE's training system, and more than a little about operations. They knew in person many of the agents deployed into France. The risk was too great. Only after Lee was himself deployed to North Africa to set up security at SOE's *Massingham* base did he learn that both were in training as agents.

Ken Macalister was commissioned as a 2nd lieutenant in the Intelligence Corps and started his agent training. He did well. Being well known to French Section, he may not have needed to train at Wanborough Manor, the initial 'filter' to weed out unsuitable potential agents, but only to complete paramilitary training, wireless operator training and Group B agent training at Beaulieu. Reports on his security-mindedness came from Robert Stebbing-Allen, who had joined SOE's Field Security group in December 1941 but quickly gained a commission.

Just as Macalister and Rée had been, Stebbing-Allen was tasked with security training for the wireless operators at Thame Park, Special Training School 52. Not surprisingly given Ken's experience of the same work, he was impressed by 2nd Lieutenant Macalister's attitude to security. Ken was painstaking in following procedures and it would be difficult to get any information out of him.

The comments on his serious approach to his mission were also telling; nothing would allow him to deviate from his path. But the highly strung nature that had been noticed at university was still occasionally evident here. Although resourceful, he needed to be under strong leadership when under mental stress. This, along with the intellectual curiosity that enabled him to master the complications of message encoding and decoding, made him more suited to the role of wireless operator than circuit organiser.

As Ken came towards the end of his training, at the Group B agent school at Beaulieu, Lieutenant Geoff Holland gave a perceptive analysis of his character and motivation. Holland had been one of SOE's first Field Security personnel, joining 63 Section as it formed in mid-January 1941. His early duties, as a corporal, included the security of the Beaulieu training schools. Along with fellow Spanish-speaker Dick Warden, he was concerned with the security of Spanish trainees living at 'The House on the Shore' in the Beaulieu complex, and probably checking that the local population had no idea of what was really going on in the stately home's grounds. Commissioned on Christmas Eve of that year, he continued working as a Field Security Officer attached to the training schools until posted to SOE Cairo in mid-1943.

In his report in Ken Macalister's personal file, Holland suggested that Ken's 'impression of easy-going urbanity' was deceptive, concealing 'a particularly tough scholar's mind, logical and uncompromising in analysis'. Ken was the type of man who 'analyses a situation, places it in relation to the wider background of the development of mankind, arrives at the only solution of the problem by deductive reasoning, and then pursues it with unswerving intellectual conviction'. His 'idealism was based on ideas rather than instinctive love of country' but none the weaker for that. Ken saw 'the German menace as a canker which calls for drastic surgery and consequent willingness for sacrifice on the part of those who are the instrument of it'.[34] The words were prophetic.

Getting There

As we saw from Teddy Bisset's involvement on *Operation Guillotine* in Chapter 1, using small seagoing craft was an important means of delivering or recovering agents and Resistance fighters on the west coast of France. This was especially the case in SOE's infancy in 1940-

---

34 TNA HS 9/954/2.

41. As the 'new kid on the block', SOE had the lowest position in the priority list for scarce aircraft. But sea transport had its problems too. One of SOE's early interests in the French coastal regions was to deliver short, sharp blows to the Germans in *coup de main* operations. As in other areas, the disruption caused by these raids, and the German reaction to them, cut across the interests of SIS. The espionage service needed a calm environment where its agents could pass unnoticed. The last thing SIS wanted was a manhunt, and SIS generally had the influence in Whitehall to make sure that its interests took priority. In any case, SOE also needed to get agents further inland. Air delivery – either by air landing or *parachutage* – became the preferred method in France.

The flavour of SOE's air operations is captured in the film *School for Danger*,[35] made by the RAF Film Unit and released in 1947. It stars several SOE agents, staff officers and *résistants* as themselves, including Harry Rée, and is 'of its time' in terms of acting. Not quite a James Bond film, but it includes reconstructions of clandestine operations into France that the written word cannot match.

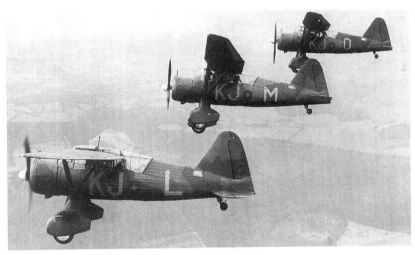

Westland Lysanders

---

[35] Also known as *Now It Can Be Told*. View online at YouTube: https://www.youtube.com/watch?v=sXHNdUM2VNY.

The only two-way means of air transport was a landing.[36] The most versatile aircraft for this mission was the Westland Lysander, which, with a landing speed of about 50 knots, could use a grass strip of 300 metres or so for landing and take-off. It carried two – and occasionally a very cramped three or even four – passengers behind the solo pilot. Several hundred passengers were carried in each direction by Lysander between England and France during the course of the war.

The air landing operations into the Loire Valley were managed by Henri Déricourt, a controversial character. French Section at first rejected evidence of Déricourt's treachery. He was doing too good a job in organising the flights. In fact, he was giving details of the air landing operations to the *Sicherheitsdienst* and allowing them to copy the personal mail transported to and from agents by the aircraft.

161 Squadron pilots with Station Commander

---

[36] An experimental system for 'snatching' a man from the ground existed by 1944. In the 1950s, the CIA developed the idea into the Fulton Recovery System. A balloon is sent aloft by the person on the ground and a modified C-130 Hercules aircraft captures the balloon's cable and the attached person.

The Royal Air Force units that carried out the skilled and dangerous task from England were Nos 138 and 161 (Special Duties) Squadrons, from 1942 based at RAF Tempsford in Bedfordshire, but with 161 Squadron having a forward operating base at RAF Tangmere near Chichester, close to the south coast, in order to make best use of the Lysander's limited range.

Arriving safely at the right landing ground depended on meticulous route selection and planning. Then, guided by three torches held by members of the reception party in an inverted L shape to show the extent of the field, and reassured by an agreed code of torch flashes in Morse code, the lone pilot would land by moonlight. The time on the ground followed a strictly disciplined procedure. The arriving passengers would step off the aircraft, those departing would approach from an agreed direction, or face the risk of being shot. They would climb on board and the pilot would be taking off again within five or six minutes.

For a larger number of passengers, the twin-engined Lockheed Hudson was used. It had a longer range and could defend itself if necessary, but of course it needed a much larger field. Alternatively, two Lysanders might be sent and the procedure on the ground had to be even slicker. On one occasion recounted by Lysander flight commander Hugh Verity, eight passengers had to be collected from a field that was too short for a Hudson. Three Lysanders were sent. The first pilot landed, taxied to the edge of the strip, called in the other two pilots in turn, watched each of them land and take off again, then himself took off. In total, he was on the ground for nine minutes.[37]

Like the air landings, parachute drops had to be made at night, timed to coincide with the full moon to allow navigation. Agents and stores were dropped from a height of about 600 feet above the ground, not so high that the wind would drift the parachute too far from the drop zone and not so low that the parachute would not have time to open. Flying at low level was hazardous in remote and hilly

---

[37] IWM Conference 27th October 1998, Oral History 18593.

regions, especially in bad weather, and even more so in areas of dense *Flak* (*Flugabwehrkanone* – anti-aircraft gun) coverage like Belgium and the Netherlands. Requests for RAF aircraft for parachute drops were always in competition with Bomber Command's campaign of night raids on Germany. SOE was never allocated as many sorties as it would have liked, until US Army Air Force (USAAF) aircraft began to become available.

From June 1944, the Germans were in retreat and the Allies had achieved air supremacy over France. It became possible to schedule drops of weapons and stores by large formations of American aircraft in daylight. An unverified tale, recounted at an Imperial War Museum conference, describes a formation of USAAF Flying Fortresses that dropped some 300 containers of arms and other supplies to an SOE circuit in the Jura. An extra aircraft joined the tail end of the formation. The Standard Operating Procedure if a bomber became detached from its formation was to join any formation the crew spotted and bomb its target. Fortunately, the crew noticed in time that the aircraft ahead were dropping parachutes and desisted from bombing the drop zone.[38]

Into France

In June 1943, Ken Macalister parachuted into a moonlit field and a complex political situation.

The French political landscape with respect to resistance was not as straightforward as popular films and books might have us believe. According to Robert Gildea:

> To deal with the trauma of defeat, occupation and virtual civil war, the French developed a central myth of the French Resistance ... It was a founding myth that allowed the French to reinvent themselves and hold their heads high in the post-war period.[39]

---

[38] IWM Conference 27th October 1998.

[39] *Fighters in the Shadows: a new history of the French Resistance*, Robert Gildea, 2015.

We should not imagine that the word 'myth' implies untruth, but de Gaulle's narrative of a France that had liberated itself without significant international help minimised the role of foreign resisters and Allied support. The reality was more complex.

Many French citizens had immense respect for Marshal Pétain, the First World War hero who had brought a sort of peace by agreeing an armistice with the Germans in June 1940 that left part of France unoccupied. Pétain's authoritarian Vichy regime cooperated with the Germans and had a degree of autonomy, until the German extended the occupation to cover the whole of France in November 1942. Moreover, Churchill's resolute insistence on sinking the French fleet at the port of Mers-el-Kébir in July 1940 did nothing to enamour the British to the French.

The first priority of the majority of a population under foreign occupation is to survive. Again according to Gildea:

> The French divided between those who collaborated with the Germans, those who resisted them, and those in the middle who resigned themselves to the situation and 'muddled through'.

Early in the war, most French people were by no means pro-British. Even to contemplate aiding resisters, hiding Jews or smuggling Allied aircrew to safety required a calculation of the risk to oneself and one's family. Taking this risk was itself heroic. Active resistance was a much more radical and dangerous step.

From the outset, though, a small French minority were unwilling to accept the yoke of occupation. Their motives were various. The simplest division is between the Gaullists and the Communists, but individuals' reasons were often more personal.

Communists had an eye on post-war power, but there were also aristocrats and young patriots who felt that the honour of France had been besmirched and something must be done to restore it. Some had experienced a personal humiliation by the occupiers and decided on the spot to fight back. Some were Jews who knew the view of their race in Nazi ideology. Some were young men who wanted to avoid forced labour in Germany and fled to the hills to join what became the *maquis*. Whether actively fighting or simply hiding someone, resisters were often coldly resolute in their determination.

Thus resistance grew slowly, despite Hugh Dalton's ambition for SOE to foment a workers' revolution in occupied countries. Political leaders in Allied capitals, impatient for results, did not recognise how long it might take to develop and train a Resistance movement. But the daily experience of life under occupation and recognition that the Allies were gaining the upper hand led to a steady growth of a spirit of resistance, especially from the winter of 1942/43.

The growing scale and confidence of the Resistance, however disunited it may have been, led to an understandable enthusiasm to 'do something' against the occupiers. While SOE agents were equipping and training these groups, they were also trying to hold them in check. The desire to commit acts of sabotage had to be tempered with prudence and careful planning, if only from a pragmatic viewpoint. The danger of reprisals was always present and a harsh reaction to sabotage could increase French resentment of the Resistance fighters.

In June 1944, though, the gloves were off. By then, a substantial Resistance movement existed in many parts of France: well-motivated, partly armed, partly trained but far from unified. SOE worked with any group that wished to undermine the occupation and did what it could to get the groups to fight the Germans rather than each other. The Resistance played a significant role in preventing the *Wehrmacht* from repulsing the Allied advance after D-Day. SOE's French Section had a major part in motivating, arming and training it.

Ken Macalister was an agent of what I have so far called 'French Section' of SOE, but it is better named the 'Independent French Section' and was known as 'F Section'. It recruited agents who were not attached to Charles de Gaulle's movement in London, which in theory had first call on 'pure' French individuals arriving in Britain. A separate SOE section, known as RF (which could be construed as meaning *République française*), was set up to liaise with and support the Gaullists.

Without even taking into account SIS and the Political Warfare Executive, six clandestine groups were operating in France as part of SOE. Apart from F and RF, a small, discreet and admirably secure section known as DF worked on clandestine communications and escape routes; it was led by F Section's former head, Leslie Humphries. Its role was to set up escape lines, generally through Spain, for agents and Allied aircrew. One of its members, Brian Walmsley, had been a peacetime actor and Modern Languages scholar at St John's College, Oxford, before becoming 63 Section's Field Security Officer. A skilled photographer, he formed and ran SOE's Photographic Section but wanted a more operational role. His skill in Spanish was relevant for the DF Section, to which he transferred. He worked on Clandestine Communications, escape routes for fleeing agents. In late 1943, he became DF's representative at the secret SOE base in North Africa known as *Massingham,* and later moved to Seville under diplomatic cover, where he briefed agents, housed them safely and moved them clandestinely across Spain.

Another section, EU/P, existed to support Poles in France and elsewhere outside Poland; half a million Polish workers were working in mines in northern France. A section known as AMF sent hundreds of agents into southern France from *Massingham.* Finally, there were the three-man Jedburgh teams, most of whom were held back from deploying into France until a bridgehead had been firmly established in Normandy after the landings on 6th June 1944.

Betrayed

Ken Macalister's arrest apparently resulted from a routine roadside check, but it was part of a German counter-intelligence process that led to the capture of several agents and hundreds of Resistance fighters. The circumstances are still controversial.

As in the Netherlands, the *Sicherheitsdienst* in Paris developed sophisticated means of detecting, infiltrating and disrupting Resistance networks. Routine document checks, radio direction-finding, double agents, bribes, informers and prisoner interrogation played their part in a multi-layered counter-intelligence framework.

Countering this system required secrecy, courage and careful adherence to security procedures, not always the highest priority for Resistance fighters and agents in the field.

Henri Déricourt, field name *Gilbert*, appears to have been working for both sides, with the aim of maximum profit for himself. His information about Lysander and Hudson operations in his area allowed the *Sicherheitsdienst* to track arriving agents after landing, even if not always successfully. As importantly, family details and information about SOE personalities in Britain, gleaned from personal mail handed over by Déricourt, were subtle tools used by German interrogators. Captured agents could be persuaded that the Germans already knew everything they needed to know. There was no point in holding out.

The infiltration and betrayal of the network into which the unsuspecting Ken Macalister parachuted was under way before his arrival. The Paris-based *Physician* circuit was led by the Anglo-French SOE agent Francis Suttill and was often known by his personal field name, *Prosper*. This legendary, but ill-fated, network suffered the arrest of hundreds of Resistance fighters when it collapsed. Much has been written about it and conspiracy theories abound; I will not enter the fray.[40] However, the story bears on Ken Macalister's fate.

It seems clear that the Germans already had a great deal of information about the *Physician* circuit, but information gained from the arrests on 21st June, including the letters, crystals and codes found on Pickersgill and Macalister upon their arrest in Dhuizon, were probably the trigger for the collapse of the circuit. SOE agent Gilbert Norman was captured in the early hours of 24th June, together with false documents identifying other members of the circuit. Further arrests ensued, including that of Francis Suttill. Norman appears to have cooperated with his interrogators, giving information that would

---

[40] Many books are in print about the collapse of *Physician*. I have found a journal article by M R D Foot and Suttill's son helpful and the latter's more recent book tells the whole story (*SOE's 'Prosper' Disaster of 1943*, Francis J Suttill and M R D Foot, 2011, *Shadows in the Fog: the true story of Major Suttill and the Prosper French Resistance network*, Francis J Suttill, 2014).

help in the arrest and interrogation of others and travelling with German troops to uncover weapons caches. Which of us can claim we would have been better at withstanding interrogation, especially when shown photostats of letters home and reports to London? Or plausible evidence of a German agent in Baker Street, in fact non-existent. The German officers in Paris had plenty of intelligence, obtained via Déricourt or from the *Englandspiel* in Holland, that they could use to convince captured agents.

Excessive trust in comrades who were carrying back detailed reports and personal letters played its part, as did a more general lack of security. The centralised Gaullist groups with whom RF Section worked were often considered highly insecure. The Communist groups to whom Suttill supplied arms were extremely cautious and maintained secure cell structures. Suttill's *Physician* circuit probably fell somewhere between the two. By the time of the disastrous collapse, *Physician* had grown very large, with several sub-circuits across northern France. Small discrete cells of *résistants*, unconnected with each other, were the exception rather than the rule. Some 'safe' apartments and houses became known to large numbers of individuals. Moreover, members of the circuit habitually met in a Montmartre cafe to socialise and play cards. The men and women of the Resistance, and of SOE, were courageous but not infallible. They had human needs in their lonely situations and were susceptible to psychological tricks.

The principle emphasised to trainee agents at Beaulieu was to hold out for forty-eight hours after arrest, in order to give other agents time to disappear. Most of them did this with astonishing courage and often for a great deal longer, or died in the process. On deployment, agents were given a range of tablets of different colours for different purposes: A, B, K and L. A was for airsickness, B was Benzedrine to keep an agent awake for long periods, K was a morphia pill that would put an average-sized man to sleep for about four hours; it was only recommended for offensive purposes. Finally, they were offered the 'L'- (for Lethal) tablet, which would cause death within seconds if sucked. Not all accepted the offer, and its use, by those who did take it into the field, is almost unknown.

Macalister and Pickersgill were questioned in the town of Blois, then transported to the Fresnes prison in Paris. From time to time, they were brought to the *Sicherheitsdienst* headquarters in the avenue Foch for interrogation. Like Francis Suttill, the two Canadians resisted interrogation and torture for several days, hoping to protect any comrades still at large from arrest.

Yet Ken was helpless to prevent his usefulness to the *Sicherheitsdienst* in another way. His radio set, eventually with other sets, was 'played back' to London by radio expert Josef Goetz, after German Signals NCOs listening in the adjoining cell were able to learn his transmission 'fingerprint' – his 'fist' – from the Morse key they had lent him to practise with. They already had his codes and the 'bluff' and 'true' checks that would authenticate his identity. As a consequence, a *Sicherheitsdienst* man called Josef Placke was able to impersonate Frank Pickersgill and set up the *Archdeacon* circuit in Alsace that Frank and Ken had been intended to form. Placke successfully ran the circuit for ten months; it was supplied by SOE with arms and equipment, and further agents who were immediately arrested. At what point F Section recognised the deception, and continued the supply drops to hide their suspicions, is unclear. It was a gradual process and F Section head Maurice Buckmaster was particularly reluctant to accept that something was amiss.

Various checks were made, but none was conclusive. The litmus test was a request from London for a conversation with Pickersgill by 'S-Phone', a short-range radio that allowed two-way communication between the ground and an aircraft. Meanwhile, Pickersgill and Macalister were in Germany, hundreds of miles away; Frank had killed two guards in an escape attempt in Paris.

Josef Kieffer of the *Sicherheitsdienst* tried to persuade Pickersgill to return to France and speak on the S-Phone. He refused. Another captive SOE agent, John Starr, said he would consider taking his place. At the last minute, he too refused and Kieffer was forced to substitute one of his German subordinates for Pickersgill. On 8th May 1944, when F Section officer Gerry Morel in the aircraft heard 'Frank Pickersgill' on the ground, he immediately recognised a German accent. The suspicions were confirmed.

Ten days later, Kieffer brought Frank Pickersgill and Ken Macalister back to Paris and tried with good food and alcohol to persuade them to cooperate. They again refused, and were returned to Fresnes prison, joining captive Resistance leaders and fellow agents like Forest Yeo-Thomas, Harry Peulevé and Maurice Southgate. After the Allied invasion on 6th June 1944, people like this were seen as too dangerous to keep in Paris. In early August, they were herded out of the prison and taken on an arduous journey that ended days later at Buchenwald concentration camp. On 14th September 1944, with his friend and compatriot Frank Pickersgill, John Kenneth Macalister was brutally executed.

Brothers in Arms

The stories of those SOE Field Security people who themselves became agents are not all as tragic as that of Ken Macalister. Ken's friend Harry Rée also parachuted into France and made a highly important contribution without being captured. He survived the war to continue his interrupted teaching career.

Harry Rée playing himself in the film *School for Danger*

Harry Rée joined SOE's Field Security group because of his elder brother Eric, usually known as 'Farmer' Rée. Eric had been a farmer in Britain for four years before renting a farm near Bordeaux in 1932. He had escaped to England with his family when the Germans invaded in 1940. He looked the part: heavy frame, impressive moustache, ruddy complexion, everyone's uncle. Eric reappears in the next chapter.

Eric and Harry came from a large Manchester family, with the 'mongrel' background – in their case Danish-Jewish-German-French-American – of the kind many of us in Britain enjoy. After attending the independent Shrewsbury School and St John's College, Cambridge, he trained as a modern languages teacher and taught French and German at a boys' school in southern England. For political rather than religious reasons, he had been a conscientious objector since his Cambridge days. By the time his call-up was activated, though, he had become convinced that political objections to fighting Germany did not hold water, and he agreed to serve anywhere necessary.

By now married to Hetty, Harry trained in the field artillery for six months before transferring to the Intelligence Corps. Intelligence training at Winchester and Matlock led to service in a port security unit at Port Talbot in Wales. Soon, though, he received a letter from Eric, suggesting that he might find the Top Secret work Eric was doing rather more interesting. Eric put a word in for him. He came to SOE for interview and rescinded his application for a commission. On 18th October 1941, Harry joined SOE as a Field Security lance-corporal.

Like many of the NCOs of lowly rank in Field Security, Harry was thoughtful and intelligent. He and Ken Macalister enjoyed working together, training wireless operators in the security-mindedness that might keep them alive. It was during this period that Harry met up with his old friend Francis Cammaerts, with whom he had shared pacifist convictions. Francis' brother had been killed in the RAF and he was thinking of throwing up his pacifism and joining the RAF.

Harry persuaded him that SOE would be a better outlet for his talents. Cammaerts went on to become a successful and naturally cautious agent. He set up a very secure Resistance circuit in southeast France, isolating it from the compromised network he had found on arrival.

Both Harry and Ken found the wireless security work frustrating. They felt their French was at least as good as that of the students in their charge and they wanted to be of use in France. A first step for Harry, given Peter Lee's opposition to his deployment, was a move to F Section as a conducting officer, accompanying Francophone trainees as they progressed through the twelve-week process. In the autumn of 1942, Lee's objections were overruled and Harry's application for agent training was approved. He started at Special Training School 5, Wanborough Manor, on 14th September, although he had little need for that phase of training. His personal code name for the operation was *Stockbroker*.

Moving on to paramilitary training in Scotland, Harry excelled. He was not thrilled about having to do the training again that he had completed as a Field Security NCO accompanying trainees. But he had 'physical and moral courage to an unusually high degree', said a report in his personal file. He spoke good French and 'school-standard' German. A sportsman and athlete, he was 'easily the fittest on the course'. He was also 'popular at all times' and displayed 'good leadership', but was 'a little impatient with his assistants and does three men's work himself'. He was a good mixer, reported one of his former Field Security colleagues accompanying the group, and 'inspires confidence and works very hard'. He was an 'extremely good influence on the other trainees' and had been 'very useful in helping to keep another student in hand'.[41]

There was a sting in the tail, though. Harry had 'a habit of leaving his private papers and money lying around' but otherwise his 'security was probably good'. His final report showed that he had done extremely well and was very keen. One comment from Scotland

---

[41] TNA HS 9/1240/3.

would not have served him well in the more conventional military but could be seen as a compliment in SOE: he was 'apt to lose his "sense of military hierarchy" in the face of incompetence or neglect of duty on the part of his superiors'.

By now he had been commissioned as a 2nd lieutenant. Parachute training at Ringway and industrial sabotage training at Special Training School 17, Brickendonbury Manor, under the imaginative George Rheam, passed quickly and successfully. The Finishing School was a different matter. His report from Beaulieu was mixed, to say the least, if not even contradictory. Harry was seen as erratic, careless and nervy, but he was also intelligent, idealistic, hard-working and had a 'strong character and a deep sense of honour'; he had 'certain powers of leadership and would win the respect of those who understood him'. The report rightly surmised Harry's apprehension about the mission he was about to undertake and about his command of French. Beaulieu recommended that 2nd Lieutenant Rée should not be deployed. F Section rejected the advice. Operational briefings followed.

Harry's primary mission was to sabotage the Michelin tyre factory at Clermont-Ferrand in central France, together with a number of secondary industrial targets in the region: electrical transformers, railway lines, other factories. He carried false papers identifying him as Henri Rayon. His field name was *César*. He was tasked to work as deputy to another agent in the area, Brian Rafferty, field name *Aubretia*.

Ready for deployment in January 1943, Harry made several abortive attempts – and bade the pregnant Hetty farewell several times – before he was finally able on 14th April 1943 to parachute on to French territory. But he was not in Clermont-Ferrand. For reasons he did not fully understand, SOE had decided to drop him near Tarbes, in the foothills of the Pyrenees mountains in southwest France near the border with Spain.

Ironically, as he had insisted on parachuting to a reception party rather than dropping blind and making his own way to safety, Harry saw no sign of a reception. He and his drop companion Dédé (field name *Samuel*),[42] a young wireless operator from Mauritius, lay low in the forest for twenty-four hours and were eventually able to make contact with the local *résistants*, led by SOE agent Maurice Southgate, field name *Hector*. Harry travelled by train with *Hector* to connect up with the comrades in Clermont-Ferrand with whom he was planning to work. But when he met his new circuit organiser in Clermont-Ferrand, Brian Rafferty, Harry's British accent in French became an issue. Rafferty decided that the risk of Harry being caught in the urban environment of Clermont-Ferrand was too great. They abandoned Harry's mission to sabotage the Michelin factory. Once again he made a risky train journey, this time with Rafferty, to 'nurse' a newly established circuit in the Jura on the eastern side of France near the Swiss border. After introducing Harry to local contacts, Rafferty left him to get on with it.

Harry worked with the Resistance in the Jura to arrange parachute drops of arms and to coordinate the different groups. The rivalry in London between the British-run support of the Resistance (F Section) and de Gaulle's 'London French' activities (RF Section) became pointless on the ground in France. Harry made sure that, in his area at least, F Section arms reached the French Resistance groups that often felt starved of support.

When Brian Rafferty visited Harry again, a few weeks before his own arrest, they agreed that potential existed for Resistance activity north of the former demarcation line between the German-occupied zone and the Vichy Government's area. While staying in contact with the Jura, Harry Rée was to set up a circuit based on the town of Montbéliard in the Doubs *département*, coordinating and supporting the few existing Resistance networks there.

After Rafferty's arrest, a new chief arrived to lead the *Acrobat* circuit in the Jura. This was John Starr, who established himself in a comfortable *château*. Harry was to work under him, but 'disliked

---

[42] This was Amédée Maingard, who later founded Air Mauritius.

Starr's assertive manner [and] did not fancy the new circuit secure'.[43] Starr gave Harry various tasks, including trying to train *maquis* who were disorganised and ill-disciplined.

Both in the Jura and in Doubs, Harry stayed with local families who were proud to be helping the war effort, risking their lives to shelter him. After the war, he broadcast on BBC radio about these unsung heroines and heroes. In early May 1943, he had been sitting in a peasant cottage with one of these families, listening avidly to the '*messages personnels*' that came out on the BBC French Service every evening. He was listening for a particular sentence that he had pre-arranged before leaving England. It came: '*Clémentine ressemble à sa grand-mère*' (Clementine resembles her grandmother). Thus he learned that his first child, a daughter, had been born that day.

Travelling around the area by bicycle, Harry set about arming and training the Resistance groups. On one occasion he was stopped by *gendarmes* as he cycled along a country road with an explosive charge in his saddlebag. Mercifully, they did not look further when he showed them the pyjamas on top of the charge.

Helped by his Field Security training and extensive experience of teaching other agents how to stay secure, Harry was cautious. Soon after he settled in Doubs, his chief, John Starr, was betrayed by a traitor, who also tried to lure Harry to a meeting. This man continued to menace the security of the circuit until he was tracked down by the Resistance and killed on 9th November 1943. In the clandestine world, justice was rapid and brutal.

After the arrests, Harry pieced together his own circuit, known as *Aubretia* but later named *Stockbroker* after Harry. His aim was to carry out relatively modest acts of sabotage, particularly on the railways, so that the saboteurs would be competent and confident enough to cut the railway lines through the Belfort gap when the Allied invasion came. When the expected *parachutage* to his groups did not come, he managed to get some parachuted arms and

---

[43] *SOE in France: an account of the work of the British special operations executive in France 1940-1944*, M R D Foot, 2006, p 256.

explosives sent over from the Jura. He supplied railwaymen with charges that could be attached to railway engines and trained them in their use.

Harry Rée's most important sabotage contribution, though, related to the Peugeot factory at Sochaux, which was manufacturing tank turrets, aero engines and other machinery critical to the German war machine. At the time, Peugeot was a family business. Harry was put in touch with young Rodolphe Peugeot, initially to borrow money that John Starr had requested, and got on well with him.

Soon afterwards, an RAF bombing raid on Montbéliard and Besançon achieved no damage to the factory, but caused over a hundred civilian casualties. The local people took this stoically, accepting the risk to them of the war being prosecuted against Germany, but it set Harry thinking. Surely if he could arrange sabotage at the factory, such bombing raids would be unnecessary.

Harry Rée became convinced that bombing of factories in France by the RAF, even though they were supplying the German military, was counter-productive. The negative consequences for French civilians would be far fewer if the factories were sabotaged by the French Resistance. He approached Rodolphe Peugeot, who enthusiastically agreed with the proposal and agreed that Harry could contact factory foremen who would know how to inflict critical damage. The firm's chief electrician gave Harry a tour of the factory.

Thanks to the sabotage instruction at STS 17, Harry was able to make intelligent suggestions, but realised that the factory personnel already had a good idea of how to proceed. With what Maurice Buckmaster later described as 'the courage of a lion',[44] Harry Rée organised sabotage attacks on key equipment like compressors, lathes, boring machines and electrical transformers. In his report to F Section on the sabotage at Sochaux, Harry asked them to keep the RAF from bombing the factory, which was eventually agreed, provided the agent reported monthly on the factory's production.

---

[44] TNA HS 9/1240/3.

Harry also passed a message of thanks to George Rheam, the industrial sabotage instructor at Brickendonbury Manor. German security precautions were tightened in March 1944, but not before Harry and his group in the Peugeot factory had effectively kept it out of action for five months.

When the Peugeot family were accused soon after the war of collaborating with Germany, Harry asked permission to write to the local newspapers in France putting the matter straight. The files do not reveal whether he was allowed to do this.

Harry Rée's area of operations was within a few miles of the Swiss border. After John Starr and several French *résistants* were arrested in July 1943, Harry decided to lie low and let the situation cool down for a while. He slipped across the nearby border into Switzerland, with the help of a hairdresser who was also a part-time smuggler, and presented himself to the Swiss border guards. A Swiss intelligence officer put him in touch with the British and helped him return to France a month later. Harry realised that it would be easier to send reports to London via the British Embassy in Bern, couriered by his smuggler friend, than to take them to Clermont-Ferrand to be encoded and transmitted by the wireless operator there.

Another visit to Switzerland followed a more difficult experience. One day in late November 1943, Harry set out to meet schoolteacher Jean Hauger, code name *Macout*, who led a small Resistance group made up of his pupils. When Harry arrived at the man's house, the door was opened by a member of the German *Feldgendarmerie* brandishing a pistol. The schoolteacher had been arrested and arms had been found in the house, he said.

Harry claimed he had come to borrow a book and engaged the man in conversation, even offering him a drink. He picked up the bottle and hit the man on the back of the head with it, but not hard enough. A struggle ensued, and the man fired his pistol several times. Perhaps Harry's paramilitary training kicked in, because he eventually got the upper hand and the man weakly told him to leave, crying 'Sortez! Sortez!'.

Himself exhausted, Harry ran into the fields behind the house and swam across a river, by which time he realised that he had been hit in the side by the bullets. People in the house to which he staggered called a doctor, and three days later Resistance fighters smuggled him across the border into Switzerland. Harry spent two weeks in a Swiss hospital and then remained in Switzerland from December until May. He kept in touch with his Resistance groups in France through clandestine border meetings and continued to report back to London, not just about his circuit but about France more generally. His survey of French morale, social character and public opinion made its way to 10 Downing Street in February 1944.

Thoughtful ex-pacifist agent that he was, Harry Rée had devised a means of slowing or halting factory production without the risk of civilian casualties. He was always concerned to keep the French population on side. For this reason, he did not encourage attacks on German soldiers, which would almost certainly provoke reprisals and possibly reinforcement of the region. Also, he represented himself to the French as a person under authority, who would try his best to fulfil requests but made no guarantees, to avoid raising expectations and causing resentment. The citation for his Distinguished Service Order quotes a local Resistance leader: 'Thanks to his example the area became one hundred percent Resistance-minded from the end of 1943 and did not rest until the expulsion of the enemy'.[45]

---

[45] TNA HS 9/1240/3.

Harry Rée's *Médaille Commémorative* certificate

CHAPTER 6

Fighting Back

'Now this is not the end. It is not even the beginning of the end. But it is, perhaps, the end of the beginning.'
Winston Churchill, Mansion House, 10th November 1942, after the Battle of El Alamein

The Mediterranean Front

AS 1942 DREW CLOSER TO ITS END, Britain had been doing battle with Italy and Germany in North Africa for nearly two years, in desert tank battles that ranged over hundreds of miles of the Mediterranean coastal area, without decisive victory for either side. Defeat for the Axis forces in this region would provide a springboard for the advance into Europe, even if it might be seen as a diversion from the main effort of a landing in France. SOE would play a major role in this offensive, but first it would have to expand from its small base in Gibraltar and the larger one in Cairo.

Cairo

SOE Cairo was responsible for activity throughout the Middle East and the Balkans – Greece, Albania, Yugoslavia – and much has been written elsewhere about these operations. At least according to its enemies in the Cairo General Headquarters, the Cairo organisation was also a security nightmare. However, this may have been a symptom of the rivalry between departments that distracted from fighting the real enemy. Overlapping responsibilities led to persistent arguments over command and control between SOE, SIS, MI5 and the local organisation Security Intelligence Middle East. As Bickham Sweet-Escott put it:

> Nobody who did not experience it can possibly imagine the atmosphere of jealousy, suspicion and intrigue which embittered the relations between the various secret and semi-secret departments in Cairo during that summer of 1941, or for that matter for the next two years.[46]

A purge in mid-1941 should have improved things, but a security issue still existed in September 1942, when Cairo requested help from the Security Section in London. The Section was starting to increase its involvement in the security of the hitherto independent overseas missions. In London, the Chiefs of Staff set SOE's policy guidelines but did not generally engage in operational detail. SOE had its own cabinet minister. In overseas theatres, this 'top cover' was not available. The local Commander-in-Chief wanted much greater control over what SOE was doing.

London sent a Major Gillson, recruited from MI5, to sort out SOE Cairo's security. Gillson was joined by Arthur Baird, who had been commissioned into the Security Section in July 1941 after six months in No 63 Field Security Section. In August 1943, the security presence in Cairo was increased by several NCOs from what had by then become a single SOE Field Security group.[47] Many of them went forward into Italy as the pace of the advance increased.

North Africa

The need to take the fight to the enemy had of course been the main reason for SOE's formation in the desperate situation of summer 1940. However, by winter 1942-43 the military pressure on Italy and Germany had reached a much greater scale and breadth. SOE's role had already changed from a political attempt to foment uprisings in occupied countries to that of building up effective armed partisan

---

[46] *Baker Street Irregular*, Bickham Sweet-Escott, 1965, p.73.

[47] They included J P Sinclair, J E Forward, G W Cottis, J G Barvis, H O J Folks and J P Marriott.

support for the forthcoming Allied invasion. Now it would have to work out how best to coordinate its action with an Army offensive.

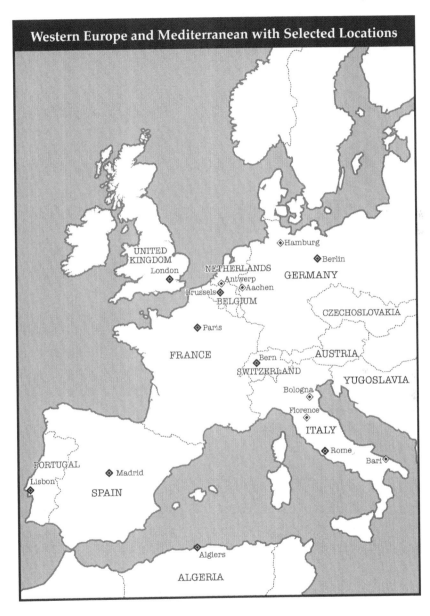

Western Europe and Mediterranean with Selected Locations

Despite Stalin's insistence, the expected invasion of northwest France – the Second Front – did not take place in 1943. Instead, the focus was on North Africa and the Mediterranean. In mid-1942, Erwin Rommel's *Panzerarmee Afrika* had advanced eastwards until halted by the Allied 8th Army in the first battle of El Alamein. It threatened the British presence in Egypt, but was defeated in November 1942 in the second battle of El Alamein and driven back by the 8th Army, now under the command of Lieutenant-General Bernard Montgomery. Meanwhile, further west, about 75,000 American and British troops carried out an amphibious assault on French northwest Africa, *Operation Torch*.

On the *Torch* eastern flank in Tunisia, SOE's *Brandon* mission helped to obstruct and subvert the Vichy French and Germans. Vichy French forces were in North Africa in some strength, but their commander was eventually persuaded to cease any resistance. Days later, Hitler ordered the occupation of Vichy France. The Axis forces in North Africa were under pressure from east and west and SOE continued to support the Allied campaign with raids into Tunisia under the *Brandon* mission. This was not a great success, but it was the first attempt to integrate SOE into a major operation.

Brandon gained as its security officer John Oughton, who had joined SOE in February 1941 as a member of 64 FSS before being commissioned into the London Security Section in September 1942. He had taught French before the war and worked as an accompanying security NCO for French Section, but he also became an instructor for the Polish Section at Special Training School 43, Audley End House. As the North African campaign drew to a close with the surrender of all Axis forces in the region in April 1943, *Brandon* was subsumed into the more substantial *Massingham* mission and Oughton joined Peter Lee and Eric 'Farmer' Rée in trying to keep it secure. The Allies had established a North African stronghold and could contemplate advancing into Italy and beyond. The pace was quickening.

Massingham

'Farmer' Rée travelled to Africa by sea, his boss by air, as his rank warranted. But Peter Lee arrived four weeks after Rée and the Field

Security men under his charge. The difficulty in getting an air passage was that fierce.

Gubbins had tasked Lee with the security of the new forward base in North Africa. He was to put together a group of Field Security men and take them with him. He selected a group from among those who could speak French or Italian and put 'Farmer' Rée in charge. By now, Rée had been promoted to company sergeant major.

While Rée sailed with his team in March, Lee waited for nine weeks for a seat in an aircraft. Only after an aircraft carrying actor Leslie Howard was shot down did the queue for seats miraculously shrink. Lee travelled with KLM via Lisbon, sitting on canvas seats, and was amazed to see a bustling, undamaged city with lights blazing at night: no sign of the blackout he had been used to in London. And there were bananas, oranges and real coffee, things he had not tasted for three years.

Lee and the Field Security men were heading for Algiers. After *Operation Torch*, SOE had established a North African mission near the city, with the code name *Massingham* and the meaningless official name 'Inter-Services Special Unit 6'. This was a base for clandestine operations into southwestern Europe, complementing the operations into the eastern Mediterranean and Balkans run from the Cairo base. Part of it, the AMF Section led by Jacques de Guélis, operated agents from *Massingham* into southern France.

At *Massingham*, SOE worked in cooperation with the clandestine operations element of OSS. Initially, this was not at all welcome to OSS director 'Wild Bill' Donovan, as French North Africa was agreed to be an American area of operations. Also, OSS was at the time relying on its success in French North Africa in its battle for survival in Washington. When the Allied commander General Eisenhower agreed to the establishment of *Massingham* near Algiers, Donovan felt that OSS's primacy in the region was being undermined. SOE's senior staff recognised his concerns but would not be swayed from establishing a North African base. SOE accepted Donovan's insistence that OSS operations would be independent, and a formal OSS base outside Algiers was indeed established. But SOE pressed on with the plans for its new forward base and invited OSS to cooperate. A location about 20 kilometres west of Algiers, close to an airfield, was eventually chosen.

Club des Pins was a secluded group of luxurious buildings surrounded by pine trees. Today it has returned to its original role as a luxury beach resort, but in the spring of 1943 it hosted activity of a more frenetic kind. The SOE team quickly built a miniature version of SOE's British establishments: paramilitary training, parachute training, maritime operations and a finishing school *à la* Beaulieu in the Atlas Mountains.

Robert Searle, a former sales promotion manager for a printing and packaging firm who had been a member of 63 FSS, arrived at *Massingham* in July 1943. He originated in Chipping Sodbury near Bristol, had a degree in commercial law from the University of Bristol and had studied for two years in Grenoble and three months in Perugia. In October 1942, he had been commissioned from Field Security into F Section as a conducting officer, accompanying trainee agents through the three-month 'round' of courses. He spoke French and Italian, and his experience was put to good use in the more concentrated *Massingham* training system. He took on responsibility for all students, as well as liaising with the French High Command.

An additional complication affecting *Massingham* was the difference in American and British attitudes as to which French group represented a legitimate post-occupation French administration. Perhaps against his own instincts, Churchill had put his weight behind de Gaulle, who had growing support among the occupied French population. Roosevelt disliked de Gaulle and favoured either General Henri Giraud, de Gaulle's rival, or Admiral Jean-François Darlan, the commander of Vichy French armed forces, who had ordered his troops to cease resisting the invading Allies in *Operation Torch*.

The agreement between Darlan and General Mark Clark, which had led to this ceasefire order, strengthened the Vichy hand in North Africa and led to the marginalisation and even arrest of de Gaulle's sympathisers there. It was very unpopular among French Resistance fighters. To Eisenhower's fury, a Gaullist French officer shot and killed Darlan on Christmas Eve 1943, using a weapon supplied by SOE. The continuing competition for leadership of the Free French movement, between de Gaulle and Giraud, was a cause of discord between the USA and Britain, and a source of constant irritation for *Massingham*. It was only partially resolved in June 1943, when Giraud and de Gaulle cooperated in a Committee of National Liberation that was progressively dominated by the latter.

Churchill and de Gaulle, 1944

At the operational level, Anglo-American cooperation functioned quite well, including formation of a combined Special Project Operations Centre. Whatever official perceptions had to be maintained in Washington, the British officers on the ground were determined to work hand-in-glove with the Americans. The SOE detachment was led by Douglas Dodds-Parker. Another Douglas, film star Douglas Fairbanks Jr, proved an amenable individual on the American side, even if Anglo-American cultural differences always bubbled under the surface. The British felt that the inexperienced American organisation had little idea about agent recruitment, training or security; the OSS officers felt that they were being controlled by snooty Brits who saw themselves as superior.

Nevertheless, the two organisations at *Massingham* were by May 1943 working effectively together and contributing according to their strengths, an example of constructive Allied cooperation that was not always evident elsewhere. Massingham became the most active and important SOE base outside Britain, providing special operations support to the Allied invasions of Corsica, Sicily, mainland Italy and southern France.

Peter Lee and his Field Security Detachment, under Eric Rée's avuncular control, were tasked with keeping the new establishment secure, with the 'help' of a group of Spanish Communist guards who had been liberated from a concentration camp. Physical security was a potential problem. A German submarine in the bay would have been able to wreak havoc among the radio antenna arrays. Mercifully, it did not happen.

Most files at *Massingham* were destroyed when the base was closed down, so information is only available about one of the men who accompanied Farmer Rée on the ship to Algiers: Sergeant F H J B Morris.[48] Fred Morris was an experienced NCO who had served in 6 and 30 FSSs in the British Expeditionary Force in 1940, before joining SOE's first Section, No 63, on 14th January 1941. He had studied and worked for some time in France and had then taught at Berlitz language schools in Freiburg and Duisburg in Germany, leaving just before war broke out in 1939. He was fluent in French, German and Italian, and had been teaching himself Russian in his spare time since 1940. Accompanying trainee agents of the French, Russian, Italian,

---

[48] Others included P A Lloyd, E Beaumont, E R Saunders, R W Stokes, P T Garvin, N E Minaur and D F N Peploe.

German, Norwegian, Polish, Danish and Belgian Sections, he had completed the three-month cycle of agent training three or four times. His skills and experience made him an obvious choice for *Massingham*'s training schools.

In the summer of 1943, King George VI broke his visit to North Africa for three days at *Club des Pins*. This was a vacation break, but the king took time out to inspect and talk at length with the *Massingham* personnel. A few weeks later, *Massingham* played a major role in the secret process that led to Italy's surrender. After the tide of Italian politics had turned and King Victor Emmanuel III had ordered Mussolini's arrest, SOE set up secret radio communications between General Eisenhower's headquarters in Algiers and Marshal Badoglio, the new Prime Minister, in Rome. They asked Badoglio to 'spring' Dick Mallaby, an SOE wireless operator captured by the Italians after parachuting into Lake Como, from prison and install him in Rome to work the set.

For the duration of the secret talks, two Italian generals were brought to *Massingham* as hostages for good conduct. The Field Security men guarded the generals, but Peter Lee, a music lover, was delighted to host one of them in his villa and discuss Italian opera into the early hours.

Meanwhile, the FANYs (most of the female wireless operators were members of the voluntary uniformed First Aid Nursing Yeomanry) worked round the clock decoding the terms of surrender. The armistice was signed on 3rd September 1943 in Sicily, by now occupied by the Allies, and led to a German invasion of most of the Italian mainland.

Sadly, at 6.00 on the morning of 22nd November 1943, Eric 'Farmer' Rée died from injuries sustained in a motorcycle accident outside Algiers. He left behind a widow and three children.

Italy

As the Allies invaded Sicily in July and mainland Italy in September 1943, SOE was developing a new means of operation. No longer was it acting independently in occupied countries. Instead it was acting under operational command of the major Army formations, tasked to contact and arm Resistance forces in support of the Allied advance. Its first experience of this role had been in the *Brandon* mission in Tunisia; lessons had been learned.

Following the removal of Mussolini, and the subsequent Armistice with the Allies, Italy was no longer an enemy but a 'co-belligerent'. But this did not mean the invasion would be easy. German forces, supported by diehard Italian Fascists, mounted a very effective defence of Italian territory. Every inch would be fought over.

The first SOE mission after the Italian surrender was led by Major Malcolm Munthe. Its role was to establish contact with the thousands of anti-Fascist Italians who wanted to fight the remaining Italian Fascists and the Germans, and to channel their efforts into supporting the Allied advance. This would involve organising, arming and even training the different groups. A training school was quickly set up on the island of Ischia, giving abbreviated versions of SOE training. Progress in raising an Italian Resistance movement before Italy changed sides had been disappointing, but it now became what William Mackenzie, in his secret history of SOE, called 'in the end one of the greatest Resistance movements in the West'.[49]

Yet the Allies advanced at a painfully slow pace up the Italian mainland. General Mark Clark famously rushed to take Rome on 4th June 1944, but the Germans fell back and held a large area of the North until the end of April 1945. Munthe's mission, on the west coast at Capri, and a subsequent mission, formed at Brindisi to work with Badoglio's anti-Fascist government, were subsumed into a larger SOE force, code name *Maryland* and headquartered at Monopoli on Italy's east coast. It was designated No 1 Special Force.

The force carried out missions and raids behind the German lines and supplied arms and explosives to partisan groups in the German-occupied north. Italy during this period was a maelstrom of refugees, agents, double agents, rumours and deceit. Into this confusion came

---

[49] *The Secret History of SOE: the Special Operations Executive, 1940-1945,* W J M Mackenzie, 2000, p.546.

Peter Lee's Field Security team from *Massingham,* to provide a security element for No 1 Special Force. At the same time, Cairo was establishing a forward base in Italy to continue its operations into Greece, Albania, Yugoslavia and Austria from a closer location, under the name of Force 133. Arthur Baird, now a major, arrived as its Security Officer and Robert Stebbing-Allen, commissioned as a captain, also moved from Cairo to Italy with Force 133.

Lee had to argue his case for a security capability to be included with the SOE force moving into Italy. Security was often seen as an unnecessary distraction from active operations; it had not been thought necessary at *Massingham,* which had 'done without' from November 1942 to April 1943. For Italy, Lee won the argument. He left John Oughton behind to look after security at *Massingham* and set off for Italy.

The journey approached the bizarre. At the last moment, it was decided that the twenty or thirty headquarters staff of the *Maryland* mission would travel via Malta. The convenience of air travel from Algiers via Tunisia, and a comfortable weekend stay with the Governor of Malta, degenerated as they were presented with the rat-infested fishing schooner *Gilfredo* as their transport from Malta.

The motley group – they included a former rubber planter, a Polar explorer and the former conductor of the Vienna Philharmonic – slung hammocks anywhere they could find a space on deck. As the ship chugged across the Mediterranean, they dived into the sea once a day to compensate for the lack of washing facilities. A bucket in the hold served as a toilet and was occasionally emptied overboard. On tying up at the wharf in Brindisi, they were surprised to learn from a naval intelligence officer that they had sailed through two minefields.

Gerry Holdsworth, formerly a leading light of SOE's Atlantic and Mediterranean para-naval operations and before that an officer in the Intelligence Corps, commanded No 1 Special Force. Although Holdsworth set up his operational headquarters in Monopoli, Peter Lee thought that might attract too much enemy attention. He therefore took his security unit to Bari, 30 miles further north. Thinking it needed a name that would make sense to the Army, he called it 300 Field Security Section for cover purposes. The different goals of the operational and the security staffs often led to heated disagreement. Lee and his Field Security men wanted to be sure that agents parachuted or landed from a boat into northern Italy would not jeopardise other operations if they were captured. The operational staff found the intrusion a hindrance.

With Lee was Frank Donaldson, the sergeant who had been a member of 65 FSS and had participated in the disastrous Dieppe raid. Donaldson was fluent in German, French and Italian and had been rushed to Algiers to join Lee on the deployment into Italy. Within a few weeks, he was given an emergency commission to act as a Field Security Officer at *Maryland*.

Lee also had two skilled Italian-speaking interrogators, who could recognise regional accents and were excellent at discerning whether Italians trying to cross the lines were refugees or Fascist agents. By exploring an individual's background and history with a thirty-three-point questionnaire, the interrogators were able to discern whether he or she was 'safe', or a Fascist with a memorised cover story. The unit requisitioned a house as headquarters and took over a nearby flat for accommodation, vacated in a hurry by a German officer who left behind a hoard of expensive perfume.

Paramilitary, parachute training and 'finishing' schools were set up in and around Monopoli. Holding schools accommodated agents as they were prepared for their missions. Dozens of requisitioned villas and apartments, given names like Hillside, The Castle and Dick's Roost, housed students in the various phases of training or acted as headquarters. Fred Morris, the former member of 63 Section who had gained his experience of SOE training as a Field Security NCO and then joined the training staff at *Massingham*, became an instructor in the No 1 Special Force Finishing School and was commissioned in September 1944.

Just as in Britain and Algiers, even though the agent training was shorter, Field Security NCOs accompanied the potential agents during training to assess their character and instil the security-mindedness that might help them survive in German-occupied northern Italy.

Sergeants Beaumont and Stokes, two of the original members of 65 Section, were among those monitoring the students; they even played roles as the students were sent out into local towns to practise their counter-surveillance skills. Geoffrey Holland, who had been on the security staff at Beaulieu, joined Lee and helped with the training and screening of agents.

Although the situation in southern Italy was relatively safe, to travel across the Apennine Mountains from Bari to Naples in a requisitioned Fiat was an adventure in itself. All bridges had been blown. Military civil engineers had created temporary roads that would snake down into a steep gully, ford a stream and climb up the other side.

Apart from the physical and political chaos among the Italians after Italy changed sides, No 1 Special Force had to put up with confused and dysfunctional command and control arrangements. US/UK policy differences with respect to the Italian Resistance, especially the Communists, also caused tension. Suspicious of SOE's motives and determined to build up US prestige in Italy, OSS refused to participate in the proposed coordination of support and supplies for partisan groups.

Yet British morale was high. Even though the German front line was only 100 miles to the north and the Allies had little defence in depth in eastern Italy, the atmosphere in Bari and Monopoli was optimistic and exhilarating. FANYs arrived towards the end of 1943. They included Ruth Hermon-Smith, who was to be Peter Lee's personal assistant, and others who worked as radio operators, secretaries or conducting officers for agents. They experienced a *frisson* of excitement as they mixed with British Liaison Officers just back from deployments in Albania or Yugoslavia. The tension and tremendously hard work were balanced by a carefree social life and the occasional wild party.

The Allies were at last fully on the offensive. The groups who had come from Algiers and Cairo were running operations into northern Italy and the Balkans. In the absence of Allied resources, the Italian Air Force and Navy were actively supporting SOE's agent deployments and pick-ups in the north, using aircraft, submarines and fast patrol boats.

Peter Lee and the men of 300 FSS were busy interrogating Italians who had been arrested or captured crossing from the north. They built up a card index, eventually numbering over 40,000 cards, containing the alias, real name and description of known Italians, whether for or against the Allies. Every time the interrogators questioned someone, the FANYs and NCOs had to work through 30-40 pages of mind-numbing transcript and notes, extracting every name and description and manually transferring the information to the card index. Then data could be accessed to answer a query or to work out whether a wireless operator was transmitting under German duress, but a task that would take minutes with today's computer power could take hours or days. Slow and laborious it may have been, but the system worked. If an agent or partisan group were captured in the north, Lee was generally able to tell *Maryland* exactly which others might be compromised, so that they could go to ground.

In February 1944, John Senter, Director of Security in London, visited the Mediterranean to check on the security arrangements in Italy. As a result, responsibility was divided according to function, as in London, rather than whether the officers had come from Algiers or Cairo. Peter Lee was given responsibility for all counter-penetration work, the equivalent of the Bayswater Special Section in London, and Arthur Baird took on physical security.

The language skills of men like Frank Donaldson were often misused. Any time a task required an Italian-speaker, they would be called on, whether it was to requisition a car or apartment, speak to the local authorities or buy black market silk stockings to send home. It left little time for their real duties.

Before agents could appear for interrogation, they had to get through the lines. The US 5th Army was advancing up the west side of Italy, but the front was relatively fluid. Agents or couriers would present themselves to an American unit with a password that had been passed to them by radio, for example *San Pietro m'aspetta* ('St Peter is expecting me'), which was eventually compromised and replaced by *Giorgio se l'ha cavata bene* ('George has got away with it well'). Liaison with 5th Army counter-intelligence was good, but Lee and his men were never quite sure that inexperienced infantry soldiers would recognise the passwords. Sometimes Lee suspected that an agent expected to come through the lines had been captured and 'turned', and warned 5th Army in advance. Occasionally, the communications with Allied armies were more trivial. One Italian agent wanted to recover the field glasses, Beretta pistol and 3,000 lire of his personal money that had been confiscated by the American infantry.

An example of a case that Peter Lee's men and women had to unravel was an Italian SOE agent, field name *Apollo*. He was known to have been captured by the Germans in January 1944. When Florence was liberated in August, documents were captured showing that he had confessed to his German interrogators. By December, he had been located in a hospital in Modena and was expected to present himself to security personnel in Pistoia. 300 FSS suspected that he was a 'plant' and arranged with 15th Army Group for him to be passed through the lines to them for interrogation.

Another Italian, a wireless operator who had been a humble garage mechanic, was sent back through the lines as a double agent by the Germans after being captured in the north and forced to transmit. He reported this to 300 Section, who were inclined to trust him, as he had been transmitting the intelligence the Germans gave him, but had included brief phrases to show that it was false. As a precaution, Lee had him put in the main prison in Rome and questioned about his transmissions. How had he managed to incorporate the warnings? They were amazed to learn that through mental agility he was able to encode the phrases in double transposition code, in his head, and add them to the message under the watchful eyes of his captors. To try out what they could hardly believe, they asked a FANY wireless operator who knew the man's Morse code 'fist' to sit in an adjoining room and decode a test message sent by the prisoner, with 'spoof' phrases added. Three times they ran the test, and the young woman reported that the garage mechanic did not even falter as he perfectly incorporated a 'secret' phrase.

SOE had infiltrated agents and wireless operators into Rome to establish contact with local anti-Fascists, and kept Resistance leaders in radio contact with *Maryland* for six months. Within a week of the Italian capital's liberation in June 1944, Lee and his team redeployed to Rome, setting up their headquarters in the former offices of Mussolini's Fascist Ministry of Popular Culture. Meanwhile, SOE agents and Allied prisoners who had taken refuge in the Vatican had been able to leave. Their place had been taken by German officers, whom Lee wished to interview. Pope Pius XII would not permit this.

The unoccupied part of Italy now included Rome. Despite widespread starvation, displacement and horrific damage, Italy was trying to return to some kind of normality. The contrasts were startling. By the winter of 1944, even though the war was continuing further north, the Rome Opera was restarting. Peter Lee's unit saved money where it could, and turned a profit if possible. World-famous opera tenor Beniamino Gigli had seven cars in his garage and gave Lee a beautiful Lancia limousine and a large Fiat as unit transport.

The battlefront moved slowly north. 300 Section moved with it, establishing sub-units in key locations. One of its officers, Pat Gubbins, was close to the front line with No 1 Special Force officer Charles Macintosh as the Allies fought for Florence. The Germans were holding the city on the other side of the River Arno. With Macintosh's help, a Resistance fighter ran a telephone line over the river, through the secret medieval passageway on the mined and booby-trapped Ponte Vecchio.

Using this connection and through numerous hazardous sorties through the passage, Macintosh was able to supply the Italian partisans on the other side and coordinate Allied action with their fighting against the Germans. As the pace of the battle for Italy increased, the security risks involved in such a senior SOE officer, with all the knowledge he possessed, being captured on the wrong side of enemy lines were tacitly accepted. The operators were much more willing to throw off the security shackles and just get on with it.

After Florence was liberated, Lee moved 300 Section's headquarters there for six weeks, but then moved forward to Bologna. The German defence of northern Italy was rapidly collapsing. Surrender took effect on 2nd May 1945. In the weeks leading up to the collapse, SOE had been working to ensure that the consequent political vacuum would not lead to chaos and civil war, as had recently happened in Greece. Hundreds of Italian agents and British officers and men from No 1 Special Force were infiltrated to work with the different partisan groups, implementing 'counter-scorch' plans, code-named *Freeborn*, to ensure that the retreating Germans did not destroy key facilities like dams and hydroelectric installations. In cities like Parma, Modena and the port of Genoa, organised uprisings and partisan attacks forced the Germans to withdraw or surrender. The partisans established Committees of National Liberation in the towns and villages. When the Germans and Mussolini's rump Fascist Army laid down their arms, the Committees stepped in relatively smoothly to serve as provisional local governments. Although devastated, Italy was at peace. Within days, the war in Europe would be over.

CHAPTER 7

Invading

'*Your task will not be an easy one. Your enemy is well trained, well equipped, and battle-hardened. He will fight savagely ... We will accept nothing less than full victory.*'
General Dwight D Eisenhower, D-Day orders, 6th June 1944

The Overlord Secret

MANY ALLIED SECRETS EXISTED in the Second World War, but two stand out. One, the successful breaking of German codes at Bletchley Park – giving critical *Ultra* intelligence to Winston Churchill and the few who were cleared to receive it – remained hidden for decades afterwards. The other secret was much more short-lived: the date and location of the expected invasion of northwest Europe. On the morning of 6th June 1944, the secret was out. *Operation Overlord* was under way.

Until then, the effort that went into keeping D-Day secret was immense. A special category of information – known as *Bigot* – was associated with the invasion planning, to which only individuals on the *Bigot* list had access. Censorship of mail increased, travel restrictions were introduced and much of the south coast of England became an exclusion zone.

Deception operations, like the phantom armies of *Operation Fortitude* and the *Doublecross* system that successfully 'played back' German spies in Britain, made a major contribution. Days after the Normandy landings, Hitler was still expecting the 'main' amphibious attack to come on the Calais coast.

157

Particular security problems faced SOE. The Germans were of course aware that an invasion was imminent, but increased their efforts to find out the 'Holy Grail' of intelligence: the date and location of the assault. Successful penetration of SOE networks and capture of agents could easily lead to discovery of the secret, if they knew it.

Some, particularly those in SIS, suggested that SOE operations before D-Day should cease. This is where the good liaison by John Senter and Dick Warden with MI5, and by others in SOE with Military Counter-intelligence, paid off. The military recognised that, with support from SOE and OSS, the Resistance in France and the Low Countries might play a significant role in harassing the defending Germans. Warden was made responsible for operational security of all SOE groups operating on the Continent. In particular, the Security Section's aim, with MI5's help, was to ensure that no SOE agents were dropped into occupied territory with the D-Day secret in their heads or anywhere about them.

In response to a directive by Churchill's Cabinet to prevent leakage of information about the invasion, SOE set up a Special Security Panel in mid-April 1944, under Archie Boyle. Its role was to ensure that communications with the field, travel to and from occupied territory and SOE's procedures in general remained secure during the crucial build-up period. Radio communications were of course sent in cipher, but senior directors ensured that only essential messages were sent and that any potentially hazardous dates and place names were replaced by code words. Letters and other physical communications were subject to censorship.

SOE was also responsible for liaison with foreign military missions in London. Associated loopholes, like the carriage of mail for the missions and radio sets in their possession, were closed. To de Gaulle's annoyance, the Free French were kept in the dark until the D-Day invasion was underway.

The question of travel to enemy-occupied territory by SOE personnel was more difficult. Here a judgement had to be made, usually by Boyle, as to whether a person's deployment was essential and could not be delayed until after D-Day. In any case, anyone likely to be dropped into enemy territory before D-Day had to be segregated from the *Overlord* preparations and planning. This was extremely difficult at Beaulieu, near the south coast and surrounded by invasion preparations, so trainees were sent to more remote training schools. Other checks made sure that nobody with *Overlord* information could get into enemy hands.

As Germany might be expected to try even harder to penetrate Britain by infiltrating double agents, any agents returning or escaping from enemy territory were subjected to extra interrogation. More generally, country sections were briefed to be especially security-conscious in April and May 1944.

These precautions paid off. The *Overlord* secret remained secret. SOE went on to help the Resistance hinder German opposition to the Allied invasion.

Invading

In preparation for the landings in France, the secretive isolation of SOE from regular troops had to be relaxed. As 1944 dawned and the Allies prepared to invade northwest Europe, the British 2nd Army and 1st Canadian Army came under the command of General Sir Bernard Montgomery's 21st Army Group. SOE would have to fit into this military structure.

This represented a major shake-up for SOE as a whole and for the Security Section and Field Security personnel in particular. By this stage, the discrete sections of counter-intelligence men – Nos 63, 64, 65, 2 and 84 – had effectively been broken up. NCOs were called on individually as required from a 'pool' to accompany parties of agents through training or to investigate breaches of secrecy. This would all have to change, if they were to work alongside the conventional forces. So they were formed again into sections.

Most stayed in the UK as 84 (Home) Section, but the reconstituted 64 and 65 Sections would operate in the field as Nos 1 and 2 Special Forces Detachments, embedded in the 2nd British and 1st Canadian Armies. A new Anglo-American Special Forces Headquarters would act as the rear link for Special Operations as a whole, with interrogators from the Bayswater Special Section brought in to examine any suspicious characters who might be encountered.

Just because enemy troops in an area have been defeated, it does not mean that danger has passed. Stay-behind agents and snipers may still be in place, booby traps may have been laid, confusion will abound. Even in an occupied country, not all of the local population will welcome the liberators. For this reason, every major formation had its own Field Security Section to be the eyes and ears among the civilian population in its area of operations. But the two SOE Sections had a more specialised task. They had a roving brief: to contact the Resistance and SOE agents, to sort out genuine agents from impostors and perhaps to uncover enemy stay-behind agents. The new role for the men of 64 and 65 Sections would be very different from their previous experience.

Properly structured training had become a key element of SOE, so the two Sections assembled in February 1944 for that purpose. Few of the original members of 64 and 65 were still in place. John Clark and Dickie Bell were two who joined the new Sections from the pool of Field Security personnel.

The new 65 Section trained at Tyting House near Guildford, until then a miniature version of the Inverlair 'Cooler'. Apart from tough infantry conditioning, the NCOs were taught the skills needed to handle and question suspects and familiarised with the 'Kardex', a constantly updated and collated set of reports from SOE agents. Armed with this information, the Sections landed in France a few days after D-Day and moved forward with the advancing troops.

The NCOs included fluent speakers of French, German, Dutch, Flemish and several other languages. Key members of the Sections kept the Kardex up to date. The Field Security Officer remained in the picture about the fluid battle lines and deployed operational NCOs to seek out Resistance groups. 65 Section's first encounter was with a group of Communist fighters in Normandy, led by a formidable woman, whose security had been so tight that it did not appear in the Kardex at all.

We have seen from North Africa that the Vichy regime and those associated with it had effectively lost credibility in France. Grassroots support for the Gaullists was increasingly evident. Despite President Roosevelt's reluctance, the Allies had to recognise de Gaulle, now Chairman of the Committee of National Liberation, as the leader of French resistance to occupation.

A few days before D-Day, General Eisenhower formed the EMFFI (*État-Major des Forces Françaises de l'Intérieur*) to command the Resistance forces. De Gaulle appointed General Pierre Koenig to lead it. But this was late in the day to form a major headquarters. There was no time for 'work-up'. Lines of control were tenuous, the command and control arrangements confused. Much was left to local initiative. Nevertheless, the Resistance – and especially the *maquis* – were waiting for the order to rise up. When it came, they helped to harass and interdict the defending German troop formations. In this they were encouraged, organised, trained and equipped by SOE agents already in place, by Special Air Service units, by inter-Allied missions like Teddy Bisset's *Tilleul* and by the three-man teams known as Jedburghs.

Cooperating

It had been clear to Colin Gubbins and his staff since early 1943 that an offensive from the Mediterranean would not be enough to defeat the Axis forces in Europe. Sooner or later, an invasion from Britain into France and the Low Countries would be needed. SOE started to organise itself to support this option by coordinating Resistance forces and governments-in-exile. The initiative was given the code name *Musgrave*. A special Musgrave Section within SOE started to plan on how to build up Resistance groups in the different countries and supply them when the time came. One key element of the plan was the formation of 'Jedburgh' teams.

Although SOE and OSS were often mutually suspicious in the Far East, the Middle East and Italy, cooperation between them was somewhat better in North Africa, and especially in the Northwest Europe campaign. The Anglo-American nature of the Jedburgh plan was an indication of this, and essential in light of the general blending of Allied planning under a single commander, the role that General Eisenhower would eventually take on.

The history of the development of OSS, the predecessor of today's Central Intelligence Agency, reveals an uneasy relationship with SOE. At first, 'Wild Bill' Donovan, the originator and director of OSS, was pleased to accept the support and expertise of the Brits. In turn, SOE leaders did all they could to support Donovan's battles for political survival in Washington. OSS agents attended SOE training in the UK and were 'customers' for training at Special Training School 103, or 'Camp X'. This secret training school for clandestine operations was set up in Canada by Sir William Stephenson's British Security Co-ordination (BSC), the New York-based representatives of SIS and SOE, and run jointly by BSC, the Royal Canadian Mounted Police and the Canadian military.

American suspicion of British colonial goals met perhaps subconscious assumptions by the British of their own superiority. In many areas, the two Allies operated separately amid mutual suspicion. Unlike the demarcated British arrangements, OSS covered both intelligence-gathering and subversion, in its Secret Intelligence (SI) and Special Operations (SO) divisions, which liaised with SIS and SOE respectively. As D-Day approached, cooperation had of necessity to improve. The combined headquarters initially known as SOE-SO became the Special Forces Headquarters. But the Jedburghs represented combined operations at the level of individual soldiers.

The use of Jedburgh teams had already been planned in 1942, but it was tested in early March 1943 through a major exercise in southern England. *Exercise Spartan* was a full-scale rehearsal of an Allied invasion of the Continent. To support the 'invasion', groups of 'Resistance fighters' were established a few weeks before the exercise in 'safe houses' in towns behind 'enemy' lines – such as Aylesbury, St Neots and Bedford – with whom the Jedburghs were to make contact. *Exercise Spartan* gave SOE – under its military cover name MO1(SP) – a chance to show the regular forces how Resistance groups could be used to support the real invasion.

Jedburghs receive briefing in a London flat, 1944

Each Jedburgh team included an officer of SOE or OSS, an officer of the country concerned and a radio operator. They deployed and fought in uniform. So SOE and OSS were by now to some degree cooperating with each other. In all, 100 teams were formed and trained at Milton Hall in Cambridgeshire, mostly for France but some also for Belgium and the Netherlands. Each team would be received by an SOE agent or an inter-Allied mission already in place and work with them to equip the *maquisards* for action against German forces.

As planning developed, the increased strength of the Resistance and SOE networks led to a change of role for the Jedburghs. Instead of strengthening the Resistance in Normandy to support the bridgehead, they were to be used, as William Mackenzie puts it, as a flexible 'strategic reserve' to reinforce the Resistance anywhere in France it might be required, perhaps for long periods. They would occupy 'a position intermediate between SOE's long-term workers

and the 'striking parties' provided by the SAS'.[50] The French
Jedburghs were deployed more or less according to this plan, with
some teams chafing at the bit as they waited for weeks after D-Day. In
Belgium, the few Jedburgh teams were not used; the Allied advance
was too rapid. In the Netherlands, the opposite was the case;
Jedburghs operated behind enemy lines for long periods as the Allies
advanced slowly northwards and eastwards.

Liberating

The story of the D-Day landings, the Allied difficulty in breaking out
of the Normandy beachhead, the advance across France and Charles
de Gaulle's triumphal entry into Paris are well known. Less familiar is
the role played by the under-equipped Resistance as it rose up to
overthrow the oppressors in the towns and villages of France, often
aided and supplied by SOE agents. Militarily, this was perhaps not
hugely significant. Historians have argued over this question. The
Resistance cut railway lines, disrupted communications and harassed
troops moving to defend against the Allied invasion, particularly the
SS *Das Reich* Division. It diverted German forces from the defensive
effort into internal security and had a psychological impact on the
occupiers' self-confidence. In terms of French self-esteem it was
highly significant and probably defined post-war France.

In mid-August 1944, while the Allied forces in northern France
were struggling to overcome German defences, Eisenhower launched
the delayed invasion of southern France. This was *Operation Dragoon*,
a push northwards by American and French forces. John Oughton,
formerly a Field Security NCO with 64 Section but by now a major,
joined No 4 Special Forces Unit for the operation, providing liaison
with the Resistance behind enemy lines for the United States 7th
Army. The *maquis* were able to harass the retreating Germans and fill
the vacuum left as they departed.

---

[50] *The Secret History of SOE: the Special Operations Executive, 1940-1945*, W J
M Mackenzie, 2000, p.603.

De Gaulle was determined that *La Résistance* would be seen as a purely French affair. F Section and its agents had little interest in post-war French politics, beyond ejecting the Germans. For de Gaulle and his followers, the question of who would rule France was central. To this end, as soon as Paris was liberated he insisted that F Section agents must leave the country, even though former members of the Resistance were positive about SOE's role and extremely grateful for British support. General Eisenhower's Headquarters, SHAEF, soon moved forward to Versailles. Into this political minefield tiptoed SOE staff who needed to establish a forward headquarters, a 'Paris Mission', with the aims of identifying and 'paying off' F Section's Resistance circuits and, more importantly, continuing the clandestine war against Germany, Italy and Japan.

Dick Warden, who had been the crucial link with MI5 on the tricky cases of German penetration, was sent to SOE's Paris Mission, also known as Military Establishment 24, with a security and counter-intelligence brief. He played a part in the liquidation[51] of SOE's circuits in France, worked closely with the French *Deuxième Bureau*, the French intelligence service, and the counter-intelligence section of SIS, in the confused environment of post-liberation Paris and throughout the country.

French citizens were short of food, the country lacked infrastructure and medical support, and former Resistance fighters accused the Allies of involvement with former collaborators. Banditry continued in the regions, and pockets of support for Germany remained in some French official and commercial organisations.

France may have been liberated, but the fighting was by no means over. The country remained at war. Within weeks of *La Libération*, SOE was working with the DGER (*Direction générale des Études et Recherches* – French intelligence agency) to set up an agent training

---

[51] Not as drastic as it sounds: it entailed 'tracing the missing, settling financial claims, piecing together the story of what had really happened and drawing lessons for the future' (*The Secret History of SOE: the Special Operations Executive, 1940-1945*, W J M Mackenzie, 2000, p.715).

school at Rambouillet near Paris. *Centre 20*, as it was known, was intended to prepare agents to operate in Indochina and Germany, mostly those who had already received SOE training in the UK or at the *Massingham* base near Algiers.

Specially requested by the French to be the key British officer at *Centre 20* was Robert Searle, the former member of 63 FSS whom they had known and trusted at *Massingham*. The French were keen to establish an equivalent of 'Club des Pins' in the Paris region. Agents would be trained to undertake sabotage, to contact French prisoners-of-war and to launch *coup de main* raids in Germany. Some of them were trained at Rambouillet. Others with less experience were sent for training in England.

Selected to accompany the French students through their training in England and Scotland was Arthur Hodson, who had joined SOE as a Field Security NCO in March 1943, a married man in his 40s with three children. He had been a 'portrait painter of private means' in civilian life and had lived in France from 1922 to 1940. Before being actually commissioned, he had featured in 'a somewhat irregular visit' to the Beaulieu Finishing Schools for clandestine operations. Presumably as a security check, Lance-Corporal Hodson 'was able to travel [to Beaulieu] as a phoney officer and remain there for two days before anybody discovered his presence'. He was 'a mature man of the world with a pleasant personality', and these attributes had led to his promotion.[52]

Overall, about two dozen French agents completed training, but few actually embarked on operations. The lack of any effective anti-Nazi movement in Germany meant that no prospect existed of supporting resistance. Because of this constraint, SOE in London were dubious about the feasibility of the French plans. The French actions might also cut across SOE's existing Germany and Austria operations: the work of X Section, which had been focusing on Germany since November 1940.

---

[52] TNA HS 9/725/3.

X Section

Geoffrey Spencer had a decade of experience of Germany. The son of a Lancashire cotton representative, he had attended school in the Rhineland town of Krefeld. The family left Germany in 1936 on the 'advice' of the Gestapo, and Geoffrey joined the British Army. His fluency in German initially went unnoticed and he was assigned to the Royal Artillery, but he was eventually transferred to the Intelligence Corps.

Geoffrey Spencer, 1944

In September 1941, he was plucked from training at Winchester to join Field Security at SOE. He worked for two years as a security NCO, at first with a maritime focus. In the far north of Scotland he was responsible for the security of the 'Shetland Bus', the deceptively flippant name given to the dozens of night trips made by volunteer Norwegian sailors in small boats to occupied Norway. Spencer did not just remain ashore; he later told his son how seasick he had been. On the Dorset coast of southern England he was attached to Gus

March-Phillipps' Small-Scale Raiding Force, which mounted 'pinprick' raids on the coast of occupied France, to capture prisoners, gain intelligence and add to German confusion and anxiety. Apart from this, he did his share of 'nannying' budding agents through their paramilitary and undercover courses.

After being sent for officer training, he returned to SOE with 'pips' on his shoulders in February 1944, at first to be the Field Security Officer covering a clutch of Special Training Schools and secret research establishments in southern England. It was only as D-Day approached that his native-standard German was employed in the SOE Section where it had probably always belonged.

The German, or 'X', Section had been formed in November 1940 by taking on board the few Germany operatives of Lawrence Grand's Section D of SIS. In the early days it consisted of just four officers to cover Germany and Austria. In addition, two Field Security NCOs were commissioned to be conducting officers for German-speaking agents through their training: Lieutenants Russell and Keir. Both were founder members of 63 Section in January 1941, commissioned after a few months into X Section.

Little is known about Russell, but Allan Keir was a dour Glaswegian who was 30 years old and married with a baby daughter when he joined SOE. He was one of the first Field Security NCOs, not just accompanying budding agents through training but also instructing them in railway sabotage. Fluent in German, he had travelled extensively in Germany, Holland, Norway, Sweden and Denmark before the war as export sales manager for a manufacturer of oilskin clothing.

In March 1942, Keir was sent to the Middle East by sea as Conducting Officer for a group of Austrian and Sudeten German trainee agents. It may seem a roundabout way of approaching the extended Fatherland, but the Balkans represented one of the only feasible access routes, and SOE's Balkans operations were run from Cairo. This attempt to drop agents into Austria failed, but Keir stayed in the Middle East to represent the German Section. There, he worked in Egypt, Palestine, Syria and eventually Italy, recruiting and training agents and planning and despatching operations.

The directive for the German Section included infiltration of saboteurs, dissemination of propaganda produced by the Political Warfare Establishment and encouragement of passive resistance and sabotage by Germans and, particularly, by the millions of foreign workers in Germany. But the problem for the German Section was of an entirely different nature than for those dealing with occupied countries; Germany was a much harder nut to crack. Opponents of Hitler's regime were brutally suppressed. The very effective populist campaign in the 1920s and 30s, the Nazi Party's control of the education system, youth movements, police and armed forces, the removal of liberal politicians and activists into concentration camps or their flight into exile: all saw to it that little potential for subversion existed. SOE even treated peace feelers from apparently well-meaning Germans with great caution, on strict advice from the Foreign Office.

'X' worked with other departments like the French and Polish Sections to infiltrate organisers among the 8 million forced foreign workers in Germany. Apart from this and acts of sabotage by agents who were usually dropped alone, the Section focused on attempts to undermine German cohesion and will to fight.

For much of the war, this meant various types of often bizarre 'black' propaganda using material prepared by PWE. Malingering and desertion by German soldiers were encouraged by leaflets and bogus radio stations. As a form of administrative sabotage, millions of false ration cards were dropped to disrupt the German economy. Leaflets and stickers were distributed to undermine the morale of U-boat crews. A subversive bogus edition of the *Frankfurter Zeitung* was distributed. Forged documents were circulated to foment division and suspicion among senior Nazis, including a postage stamp showing a portrait of Heinrich Himmler instead of Adolf Hitler. Geoffrey Spencer worked on many of these schemes, even doing a little forgery himself. He and his colleagues recognised that the chances of an uprising in Germany were minuscule, but took the long view and stayed in contact with – mostly exiled – opposition groups as a resource for any post-war scenario.

Propaganda: advice to German soldiers on feigning illness, disguised as cigarette papers

Some of the bright ideas consumed resources in planning and preparation but were never carried out. Winston Churchill was enthusiastic about several of these despite X Section's more considered advice. Potential operations included *Operation Foxley*, the 1944 plan to assassinate Adolf Hitler, and *Operation Braddock*, a plan to manufacture millions of small, inexpensive incendiary sabotage packs and scatter them by parachute over industrial areas of Germany, in the hope that foreign workers would find and use them. Much time, ink and factory capacity was expended in the process, but despite Churchill's enthusiasm very few of the 'Braddocks' were ever dropped in enemy territory.

As it was almost impossible to build up clandestine networks in Germany itself, X Section operated mostly from neutral countries neighbouring the *Reich*: Sweden, Switzerland, Turkey. By the spring of 1944, though, SOE was solidly established at Monopoli in southern

Italy. Groups had moved forward from Algiers and Cairo, with a small but complete agent training apparatus, a cooperative SIS document-forging facility nearby, and a substantial clandestine transport system into northern Italy and Yugoslavia. It made sense to mount operations into Germany, and especially into Austria, from here.

The potential for anti-Nazi movements was greater in Austria than in Germany, especially as the tide of the war was seen to be turning. SOE operations into Austria were stepped up. The first major effort, *Operation Clowder*, attempted overland operations starting in the winter of 1943-44 from a forward base in the Slovenia region of Yugoslavia as guests of Tito's Communist partisans, although stirring up Austrian resistance was not a high priority for the Yugoslavs. *Clowder*'s aim was to set up a series of despatch posts for the infiltration of Austrian agents and British officers into Austria.

Frank Pickering, the former member of No 64 FSS whose fluency in German, Italian, French and Spanish had resulted in his working as an interrogator at the Royal Victoria Patriotic Schools, parachuted to the *Clowder* Mission in Slovenia on 2nd August 1944. He interviewed Commissar Kraigher of the partisans and sent back a penetrating report on Slovene attitudes to British intentions in Austria. He then made his way to a Yugoslav zonal headquarters near Solčava, a few miles from the Slovene-Austrian border, where he tried without success to reconnoitre the possibilities for stimulating Austrian patriotic action across the border in Styria.

He remained attached to the Slovene partisans in that zone, but his attempted crossing of the Drava River with them was prevented when they were dispersed by German opposition. *Clowder* withdrew in December 1944 and Frank Pickering reached Italy on 5th January 1945 after an 'adventurous journey'.[53] At the end of the European war, he was posted to the Political Warfare Executive and ended his service with the rank of major. The whole *Clowder* operation was described by official SOE historian William Mackenzie as 'a brilliant

---

[53] TNA HS 7/146, History of *Clowder* Mission.

display of gallantry, entirely without practical result'.[54] However, several Austrian agents, mostly recruited from amongst prisoners-of-war, were subsequently parachuted into Austria in the spring of 1945. Some were betrayed or captured, but others were able to contact bands of Army deserters and coordinate harassment of the determined German defenders.

Some months earlier, soon after Geoffrey Spencer joined the German Section in the autumn of 1944, its status had changed dramatically. With France liberated, German forces in retreat in the Low Countries and the Allies' sights set on a rapid victory, Colin Gubbins ordered that subversive action into Germany must have priority over other SOE activity and that other sections should render all assistance. X Section became the German Directorate, led by Major-General Gerald Templer, who had been forced to give up command of an armoured division after being injured by a land mine. The resources available and the tempo of planning and operations increased dramatically. With hindsight we can see that this effort was too little too late, but the Directorate's energy was maintained until the end.

The western German city of Aachen was in Allied hands from October 1944. In addition to opening up a supply of German uniforms and identity documents for agents, it provided new opportunities for so-called administrative sabotage. Thousands of genuine blank clothing cards were dropped in the Düsseldorf area after being obtained in Aachen on 2nd November 1944 by Special Patrol Unit 22, under Lieutenant-Colonel Hazell. This SOE unit had moved forward with the advancing front after being formed to 'liquidate' – that is, administratively decommission – Polish Resistance networks in northern France. With considerable difficulty, Hazell negotiated with the American occupiers of Aachen to be allowed to search for documents. Subsequently, SPU 22 searched other captured cities, but

---

[54] *The Secret History of SOE: the Special Operations Executive, 1940-1945*, W J M Mackenzie, 2000, p 697.

also focused on infiltrating agents through the Allied lines, in cooperation with the Special Forces Detachments.

Apart from these infiltrations, the German Directorate's main focus for Germany itself was now the recruitment and training of promising potential agents 'extracted' from the stream of captured German soldiers before they were registered as prisoners-of-war – the *Bonzos* – and put into training at Special Training School 2, at Bellasis near Dorking. While Gilbert Smith served as an interrogator at STS 2 screening potential agents, Sergeant Antoni Hartog, who had joined SOE as a Field Security NCO in July 1943, lived with the German trainees and reported on their characters and suitability for deployment as an agent. This training was highly sensitive. Local people must not catch wind of the fact that Germans who were not prisoners were in their midst, even if they were anti-Nazis.

Hartog socialised with the students, escorted them to Wanborough Manor for weapons training and to Manchester for parachute jumps. His descriptions reveal a variety of life stories: a doctor from Königsberg, who had been denounced by his uncle for comments against the regime, was imprisoned in a concentration camp and saved many lives there through operations; a sailor from Hamburg whose wife had been killed in an Allied bombing raid, but who had an intense dislike of the Nazis; an Austrian from Graz who served in France and worked with the Resistance to 'liberate' German munitions, before defecting to the *maquis;* a baker from Berlin who had been drafted into the Navy but then imprisoned for seditious statements, the sentence being only three months because he was drunk at the time.

What to do with *Bonzo* students who were unsuitable for deployment exercised the minds of SOE security staff like Aonghais Fyffe. Would they have to be sent to a 'Cooler'? Eventually it was decided that they could be kept securely at Tyting House near Guildford until any information they held could no longer damage SOE operations, then returned to life as a POW.

About thirty *Bonzos* were dropped or infiltrated into enemy territory before the Nazi collapse, mostly to carry out sabotage, about half successfully. Those who returned safely from clandestine operations or were overrun by the advancing Allies might be briefed for a further mission. But then came the German surrender. *Bonzos* who had been on operations, or who had completed training too late to be deployed, were returned to their homelands with a civilian suit and enough money to keep them going for two or three months.

Some of the German POWs were unwittingly being trained for a different purpose: *Operation Periwig*. In November 1944, the imaginative X Section started to invent a mythical German underground. If a real movement did not exist, an imaginary one might cause just as much trouble for the Gestapo. All this came about far too late to make any difference, but the plan was sound. Plant stories with Swiss and Swedish journalists. Drop supplies to an imaginary reception committee. Secrete forged documents on the body of an agent whose parachute would fail to open (this idea was abandoned). Infiltrate agents who had been led to believe their role was to contact an (imaginary) German Resistance. Five of the *Periwigs* were indeed deployed and performed their briefed tasks, unaware of their 'smoke and mirrors' nature. They all survived.

The Final Push

After Dickie Bell's first tentative Resistance encounter in Normandy, 64 and 65 Sections contacted an exponentially increasing number of Resistance groups – and rooted out impostors – as they advanced across France and Belgium. There was plenty to do. Over 100 *Abwehr* and *Sicherheitsdienst* agents were captured in Belgium in the three months after the Allies entered the country.

As attention turned to the Netherlands, the Dutch Resistance became the 'Netherlands Forces of the Interior', commanded by HRH Prince Bernhard through the Special Forces Headquarters. The Resistance fighters would thus be employed in support of the advancing armies, with the Special Forces Detachments acting as points of contact, although the memory of the *Englandspiel* meant that the Resistance were treated with some suspicion. Nevertheless, the Belgian 'Secret Army', the *Front de l'Indépendance et Libération*, *Groupe G* and other networks did a great deal to assist the Allied advance: sabotage and 'go-slow' on the railways and canals, and 'counter-scorching', especially the frustration of German attempts to destroy the port of Antwerp before retreating.

Stuart Gardiner was an Intelligence Corps officer and former telephone engineer who joined SOE in 1943, at the age of 23. Tall and heavily built, he had brown hair, blue eyes and a light moustache. He was not a member of 'our' first three Field Security Sections, but he had served time in the ranks of Field Security, specialising in port security. He had lived much of his early life in Belgium and was picked up by SOE as a potential agent while at the Officer Cadet Training Unit, after being selected by the Intelligence Corps for commissioning. Although the recruitment of agents had not progressed much from the casual 'friend of a friend' recommendation, their selection had developed from the long and expensive preliminary schools like Wanborough Manor to the short Students Assessment Board at Special Training School 7 in Surrey.

Stuart Gardiner

After volunteering for SOE and completing OCTU, Stuart was sent to STS 7, where he was found to be soberminded and intelligent, but 'a slow thinker, accentuated by a habitual sense of caution and suspicion'. He was 'security-trained and very reliable', his personality should improve greatly with training and he was particularly recommended to be a wireless operator. He survived the 'sieve' at the end of the Assessment Board, and his former military background stood him in good stead when he went for paramilitary training at Loch Morar in Scotland. Here he was thought 'disciplined and orderly', a 'cheerful comrade'. 'successful at anything where neatness is required', but 'rather immature as he has no experience of occupied Europe'. After a short parachute course, he was sent for security training for wireless operators at STS 52, Thame Park, where it was noted that he considered security vitally important. But reports from his Group B training for clandestine operations were less positive, as they were for several subsequently successful agents: he 'might make an adequate [wireless] operator if kept under firm leadership'.[55]

Stuart Gardiner was parachuted into a field in Walloon Belgium on 6th July 1944, with two comrades and twelve containers of weapons and supplies. He was agent *Diomedes*, masquerading as Henri Goyvaerts, and it was his sense of security rather than inspiring leadership that would keep him alive. The circuit organiser for whom he was to work had the task of organising propaganda throughout Belgium and of contacting the *réfractaires*, the Belgian equivalent of the *maquis*, young men who had taken to the woods to avoid conscript labour in Germany. Once the supplies had been shifted by horse- and ox-drawn cart to the well-hidden Resistance camp, *Diomedes* worked out his future plans with the leaders. He was surprised at their openness. The area was dominated by the Resistance; the few collaborators had to keep their heads down.

Accompanied by two young Belgian girls, Stuart made his way to Brussels by train, on foot and by truck. However, his radio set and crystals, which were meant to follow by courier, did not reach him for a frustrating six weeks. He established himself in the village of

---

[55] TNA HS 9/563/2.

Kampenhout, 7 miles from Brussels. Once he was able to contact London, he maintained strict security. Contact was through a *boîte aux lettres* that Stuart set up in a local cafe. Gardiner made sure that he knew nothing important of the organisation with which he was working. He was provided with four armed guards and a courier, who were always very willing to follow his instructions. In view of the very active German direction-finding, he arranged to be found a new safe location for every transmission schedule. He never transmitted from the same house twice.

Liberation: Brussels, September 1944

The British 2nd Army entered Brussels on 3rd September 1944, so Stuart Gardiner was 'overrun' by the advancing front and did not suffer the constant stress of living under cover for many months or years. But he was effective in his role and when Mentioned in Despatches he was especially praised for his sense of security.

21st Army Group advanced eastwards to the borders of Germany and, after the German Ardennes counter-offensive had failed, continued into the Fatherland itself. But Germans in the north of Holland held out until the last and only surrendered on 4th May 1945. German forces also remained in parts of eastern Belgium until early February, but the liberation of the greater part of the country allowed Special Forces HQ to infiltrate guerrillas and saboteurs from Belgium into Holland. Stuart Gardiner played his part in this, as he was recruited in Brussels by Commander Philip Johns to join SOE's Mission to Holland. The Resistance in Holland and its support from SOE had to some extent recovered from the *Englandspiel* disaster, but the part of Holland still under occupation was suffering horrific starvation and young men were still being deported to Germany. Nevertheless, railway workers mounted a sustained strike and the Dutch Resistance carried out sabotage.

John Clark and Dickie Bell of 64 and 65 FSSs were both called to Brussels in September 1944, where according to them both Sections were disbanded. Bell and Clark were both assigned to No 30 Section. They advanced through the Netherlands and Germany with the British 2nd Army, arresting Nazi leaders on the 'automatic arrest' list and others suspected of war crimes. The pair ended up in Hamburg as Germany surrendered in the first week of May 1945, but continued to hunt for senior Nazis. Dickie Bell was one of those who escorted Joachim von Ribbentrop, the Nazi Foreign Minister, after his capture in mid-June 1945, to *Ashcan*, the American-run facility for holding and interrogating senior Nazis in a Luxembourg hotel.

Confusingly, there is evidence that 64 and 65 Sections were in existence long after they had supposedly been disbanded in September 1944. Intelligence Corps NCOs were still being posted to 64 Section until May 1945. From December 1944 to February 1945, it was reported to be installed in the Dutch village of Horst, near Venlo. This was a few kilometres from the River Maas (Meuse), which marked the front line where the Allied front stabilised, after the

German surprise *Wacht am Rhein* counteroffensive through the Ardennes – the Battle of the Bulge – had run out of steam.

The Section had taken over the 'control line' behind forward troops, advancing into Germany in February 1945 in *Operation Veritable*. An arrest and interrogation report shows that on 22nd February 64 Section apprehended a Dutch 'linecrosser', who claimed to be returning from enforced labour in Germany, but turned out to be a spy tasked by the Germans to find out about the effect of V1 and V2 attacks on the port of Antwerp. It does seem that the reports by Bell and Clark of the death of 64 and 65 Sections were 'exaggerated'. Perhaps this was just a redeployment of Field Security personnel according to their language skills, which certainly happened often.

The 21st Army Group counter-intelligence plan called for 64 Section eventually to be deployed on the Dutch-German border in cooperation with several companies of the Netherlands border force: the *Grenzwacht*. Immediately after the German surrender, the Section established itself near the city of Aachen, under the command of Captain Clifford Pennison, to monitor the border for Nazi fugitives.[56]

Also confusing is the fact that 64 and 65 Field Security Sections operated as Nos 1 and 2 Special Forces Detachments, by late 1944 perhaps a more accurate description of their role. Reports on their activities under these names continued well into 1945.

While the 21st Army Group front was stationary at the River Maas and during its advance towards the Rhine, 64 Section was infiltrating agents through British lines to carry out sabotage, distribute tyre-bursters and gain intelligence. Some of these were Poles from the Lille network, transported to the British sector by Hazell's SPU 22 to be smuggled across the Dutch-German border. Although established in the US area of operations, Hazell was not permitted to infiltrate agents across American lines. Others were Dutch agents, sent into enemy territory in Operations *Cabbage I* and *II* with radios to report back on German defensive positions, with a Dutch-speaking Field

---

[56] *The Bride's Trunk: a story of war and reconciliation*, Ingrid Dixon, 2016.

Security man in a forward position to relay messages back. A party of French commandos was infiltrated north of Venlo.

Meanwhile, No 2 Detachment (65 Section) focused on positioning Dutch radio operators in the occupied northern and western parts of Holland in *Operation Martin*. They were also involved in facilitating the extraction to Allied territory of Brigadier John Hackett and 200 men, who had escaped from captivity following the failed airborne attempt to take the bridge at Arnhem.

Liberation: Dutch Resistance march collaborators through street

The Allied forces advanced across Germany towards the inevitable defeat of the Nazis, liberating prisoners-of-war, discovering appalling concentration and death camps, and often encountering desperate resistance. The SOE Field Security Sections sought out agents as the advancing troops overran them, debriefed them and brought them to safety.

Possibly the last agent to be deployed undercover in the European theatre was an enthusiastic and brave Jewish anti-Nazi from Berlin named Rudolph Becker, who took on the alias of Robert Baker-Byrne in the German Directorate of SOE. He was not a member of the Intelligence Corps, but his story is an interesting example of how the German Directorate and the Special Forces Detachments worked together.

Becker's first parachute deployment into Germany, *Operation Vivacious*, was an attempt to sabotage a factory in Berlin making parts for the V2 rockets, but he was discovered breaking in by two policemen. Deciding the mission was impracticable for a solo agent, he aborted it and escaped through Switzerland. In *Operation Branston*, his second mission, he was tasked with developing a network to carry out naval sabotage and propaganda in the Lübeck area in the far north of Germany and gaining intelligence on any plans by fanatical Nazis to carry on the fight after defeat.

Just as Stuart Gardiner had gone through months of training, briefing and preparation before his deployment, to spend only a few weeks undercover in Belgium before being overrun, SOE had made a similar investment in Baker-Byrne. Apart from two pistols and three grenades, he was armed with 250 'Submarine Battery Pills' for sabotage. Less lethally, he was also equipped with large quantities of cash, gold Napoleon coins, coffee, tobacco and Swiss watches for use as bribes, as well as three different cover identities carefully prepared by the German Directorate.

However, Baker-Byrne was not infiltrated until the early hours of 24th April 1945 and spent only a few days on his operation. He used up several days trying to locate the contacts he had been given during his briefing, but most were missing. Those he could find were keeping their heads down and were unwilling to help. The most he received was a blessing from a Roman Catholic priest. Realising that his mission had no future, he set out to reach the Allied front line, sleeping in forest plantations to avoid German units. He managed to bluff his way through one checkpoint by demanding that the soldiers stand to attention, but subsequently lost most of his equipment fleeing under fire from a guard post.

Just 3 kilometres from the British front line, by now dressed in improvised British uniform, Baker-Byrne was captured by a German infantry company. With an escort party, he was passed on to progressively higher formations. *En route*, the escort met an SS unit who had to be dissuaded from shooting him, but he eventually arrived at the *Korps* headquarters. The commander, *Generalleutnant* Sauberzweig, took a personal interest and accepted Baker-Byrne's cover story that he was a British paratrooper. He survived the days of captivity, in a POW camp then a concentration camp, not least because many German officers and soldiers were concerned about their own personal positions. Pressure from Nazi diehards prevented total cooperation, but Baker-Byrne led his captors to believe that he could influence their fates and that he had some powers of negotiation.

On the afternoon of 2nd May, *Wehrmacht* escorts collected Baker-Byrne, against *Sicherheitsdienst* objections. He was reunited with General Sauberzweig and spent two days attached to the *Korps* Headquarters, until on the morning of 4th May he was handed a pistol and sent in a white-flagged car with two German generals to facilitate the surrender of the *Korps*. They passed through the British lines to the Headquarters of 11th Armoured Division, where a relieved Baker-Byrne was able to contact one of the Special Forces Detachments, explain who he was, and eventually make his way back to Britain. Sauberzweig later committed suicide in captivity, apparently to avoid standing trial in Yugoslavia for his responsibility for SS war crimes committed there while he was in command.

Thus SOE's German Section, later as a Directorate, had been unable to achieve much operationally for most of the war, but in the end kept up the pressure until what we now know was the last minute. Adolf Hitler committed suicide on 30th April in the *Führerbunker* amidst the rubble of Berlin. On 4th May, Montgomery accepted Germany's unconditional surrender. For Germany, this was *Stunde Null*: Zero Hour.

Wind-down

After 4th May, the task for the Allied military suddenly changed from combat to occupation: freeing POWs, guarding German prisoners, feeding and housing the millions of Displaced Persons throughout Europe, reducing the daily death rate in concentration camps. 64 and 65 FSSs continued to hunt down senior Nazis. For SOE as a whole, the main task was what was then called 'liquidation' of agents and networks, redeploying members to the Far East, where the war against Japan continued, and preparing for its own post-war future.

Election poster 1945

But what future? The immediate post-war period presented a new and threatening environment for SOE itself. Whatever its leaders may have thought about the continuing need for SOE's 'services', those in power – with SIS making its own feelings clear – thought otherwise. Churchill was out of office. Hostility in Whitehall persisted. The new Labour Government instructed that SOE should be wound up without delay, which in practice meant the winter of 1945-6. Training schools were closed, staff were laid off or returned to their regiments.

Some operational work continued. Military Establishment 42 was formed as SOE's organisation in the former *Reich* to trace missing SOE agents in Germany and identify impostors, to find documentary evidence of the impact of SOE on the German security services and *vice versa*, to counter any Nazi underground groups and to carry out any special operations missions required by British counter-intelligence. Either unaware or in spite of the threat to SOE's future, it set about these tasks in the British Occupation Zone with energy. It built up a card index of potential agents throughout the British Zone for possible future special operations. It established safe houses, run by Field Security Sergeants Arthur Ronnfeldt and Antoni Hartog, for the process of rehabilitating SOE agents before returning them to civilian life in Germany, or for interrogating those who presented themselves and claimed to be agents.

Some of the *Bonzos*, German ex-POWs who had been ready for clandestine work in Germany as the war ended, were sent to ME 42. Their task, along with other agents recruited from among POWs in Germany and the Low Countries known as *Peewits*, was to go undercover in POW camps in search of Nazis and subversive plots. Other agents were recruited to be deployed into the concentration areas in the far north of the British occupation zone, into which the *Wehrmacht* had withdrawn under the terms of the capitulation. In Operations *Battleship* and *Dreadnought*, agents penetrated these areas to report on the possibility of subversion and to identify any senior Nazis who might be masquerading as ordinary soldiers.

As SOE was winding down, a reprieve was granted for a few officers to investigate the fate of agents who had disappeared into *Nacht und Nebel* (Night and Fog), the Nazi decree that Allied undercover agents should sink without trace. Vera Atkins, who as its Intelligence Officer had been a key figure in F Section for most of the war, made it her personal mission to find out what had happened to the agents who had disappeared and enlisted the help of Aonghais

Fyffe, who was by then ME 42's Intelligence Officer and working in occupied Germany with the same task.

Progressively in late 1945, ME 42 started to merge with the SIS units in Germany and had eventually handed over its activities by 1st April 1946. Back at the London headquarters, Major Norman Mott managed the final stages of SOE's rundown. Mott had been a member of 64 FSS, but was quickly brought into the Security Section office and almost as quickly, in July 1941, commissioned. His thick glasses gave him an owlish look and his infectious humour had kept the others in the Baker Street office sane during the tense nights of Luftwaffe bombing raids. He was efficient, accurate and painstaking in his work, and had progressively gained an encyclopaedic knowledge of SOE's operations and agents.

By the time the war came to an end, Mott had been promoted to major and found himself answering parliamentary and Foreign Office queries about SOE and SIS agents, as Britain attempted to disentangle the complex clandestine web of agents who had been deployed or locally employed. In mid-1946, he had the dubious privilege of being one of the last to leave SOE and 'turn out the lights'.

The heroes of this book – or at least those who survived the war – went their various ways as SOE was disbanded, remaining silent about their wartime work for years or even decades. Some of them had been planning ahead well before the time came, to put their post-war aspirations into action.

In the autumn of 1944, as the end of the war seemed to be approaching, Anelyf Rees had rekindled his interest in international affairs and economics. It was a time of optimism, of belief that the war in Europe would soon be over. The German counterattack through the Ardennes and the stubborn defence of the German homeland were still unanticipated future experiences. Rees applied to join the Foreign Office, but that organisation had not yet decided its post-war needs and meanwhile no suitable appointment could be suggested there for the bookish Rees.

By January 1945, though, he was trying a different tack. He wrote personally to Archie Boyle, expressing his interest in 'the varied schemes which are now being discussed for further experiments in international organisation': what we now know as the United Nations Organisation and the Bretton Woods institutions. In his prescient view of the economic integration of Europe, he was ahead of his time. His view of the 'prospect of a first great experiment in international government based upon a synthesis of the differing ideologies of the USA, USSR, Great Britain and France', however, may today seem naive. Viewed without our subsequent knowledge of Cold War history, it is perhaps less so.[57]

The pragmatic and well-informed Boyle feared that these possible future policies were only at the incubation stage, but he agreed to meet Rees and help him if he could. The result of the discussion was an application to join the institutions being set up to supervise the reconstruction of Germany and Austria. Again, though, Rees was disappointed. Discussion with the nascent Control Commissions for Germany and Austria revealed that little chance existed of an officer being seconded to them. Anelyf Rees moved, with wife Evelyn and daughter Susan, to a position as university lecturer in South Africa, where his son Nicolas was born. Some twelve years later, Rees became founding Principal of Renison College, set up by the Anglican Church in Waterloo, Ontario, Canada. In July 1971, he died suddenly at the age of 58.

A little is known of the post-war fate of some others. Three were of course killed during the war – Teddy Bisset, Eric 'Farmer' Rée and Ken Macalister – ironically, only the last of them through enemy action. The unfortunate Macalister was executed at Buchenwald concentration camp in September 1944. Eric's brother – and Ken's friend – Harry Rée became a school head teacher after the war and was subsequently appointed Professor of Education at the University of York. He died in 1991. The Australian George Windred worked for the Foreign Office and for ICI, travelled widely in South America and died in 1964.

---

[57] TNA HS 9 1240/7, Rees to Boyle 14th January 1945.

After John Oughton advanced through southern France with the US 7th Army, he did not see the European war through. With victory in Europe imminent, many members of SOE redeployed to the Far East; the war against Japan was now the priority. Oughton was posted to Melbourne, to act as security officer for the Australian equivalent of SOE that was by now working behind Japanese lines.

Stuart Gardiner worked for a while in the post-war Control Commission for Germany and then moved to The Hague, where he worked in the 1950s as an examiner in the Passport Control Office. These offices were of course used before 1939 as a rather thin cover for SIS officers.

Brian Walmsley was still in Seville as the war came to an end. SOE had ambitions to turn its hand to hunting down illicit German assets in Spain and Portugal, but SIS and the Foreign Office scotched the idea. SOE's future would be short-lived. Walmsley settled in Seville with his new Spanish wife and died there in 1978.

As a member of ME 42, Geoffrey Spencer was closely involved both in the post-war search for missing agents and in the infiltration of *Bonzos* into POW camps. Like Anelyf Rees, he moved to Canada; he died in Vancouver in 2015, aged 95. Aonghais Fyffe, too, had a continuing role in Germany, working at Bad Oeynhausen, the nerve centre of British occupation, and tracing the fates of agents who had disappeared. Of the post-war careers of others who have been mentioned, little is known.

CHAPTER 8

Postscript

*'Nur wer die Vergangenheit kennt, kann die Gegenwart verstehen
und die Zukunft gestalten.'*
*'Only those who know the past can understand the present and
shape the future.'*
August Bebel (1840-1913)

Oradour

ON 9TH SEPTEMBER 2017, MY WIFE AND I VISITED the 'martyr
village' of Oradour-sur-Glane in the Haute-Vienne *département* of
central France. This was where, on Saturday 10th June 1944, soldiers
of the 2nd Waffen-SS Panzer Division *Das Reich* killed 642 men,
women and children, subsequently destroying the entire village. On
President de Gaulle's orders, the village was left in its ruined state as a
reminder of the atrocity. It forms today's memorial.

We had not intended to visit Oradour. But I knew something of
the history and, when we saw a road sign as we drove south towards
the Corrèze, I suggested the detour. We had not realised what a
shocking and moving experience we would find it to walk in silence
among the ruins of ordinary buildings, dilapidated after seventy years
of weathering: the garage, the bakery, the cafe, the church into which
women and children were herded and burned alive.

Many have tried to explain the motivation behind this atrocity,
which was committed the day after a similar massacre by the same
Division in the town of Tulle in the Corrèze. There are no excuses,
but the context helps our understanding. Four days earlier, on 6th
June 1944, the long-awaited Allied invasion force had established a

bridgehead in Normandy. On its way north from southern France to repel the American, British and Canadian troops, the *Das Reich* Division was ambushed and harassed by the *maquis*, who had at last been unleashed to attack the Germans directly and openly. In retaliation for these attacks, German commanders ordered reprisals in Tulle and Oradour.

As we have seen in previous chapters, the ruthless imposition of reprisals had been a constant feature of the German occupation of France, and was successful in instilling fear in the population and an ambivalent public attitude to the Resistance. In contrast to popular understanding, the role of SOE agents was often to instil a measure of caution and prudence into Resistance fighters whose passionate aim was to attack Germans. They hoped that training and organising the fighters would enable them to act more strategically and minimise the risk of counterproductive reprisals against French communities. This moral hazard of taking violent action against the occupiers, in the knowledge that innocents would pay a price, was always part of the calculation of the best and most thoughtful of SOE agents and leaders.

Oradour-sur-Glane

The ethical questions of war and peace have never been far from my mind as I researched and wrote this book. Before this project, my thirty-year Royal Air Force service had been followed by twelve years leading a conflict resolution charity, facilitating dialogue in African civil wars. My doctoral thesis looks at cooperation between outsiders intervening to bring stability in conflict-ridden societies. I wrote my previous book, *Peacemakers*, to help Christians better understand the practicality of the Biblical phrase 'blessed are the peacemakers'.

I started on *Guardians of Churchill 's Secret Army* because I noticed a gap in the historical record, revealed as my wife Ingrid researched for *The Bride's Trunk*, which relates how her Anglo-German heritage came about. Her father was a member of No 64 Field Security Section in 1944-45, her mother a civilian in the vanquished nation. Thus I did not come to the *Guardians* project simply as a war historian, but as someone with experience of both British and German cultures and the ambiguities involved. When war comes, moral compromises are made on all sides, but the Nazi regime was an evil that had to be overcome. SOE's actions were an often unsavoury but nevertheless essential part of that imperative.

Terror

With our present obsession with terrorism, it is tempting to equate SOE's actions in the Second World War with today's international terrorists. But that would not be a true comparison. Unlike modern terrorist movements, SOE agents were not trying to strike fear in the population, just in the occupying forces. Nor were they trying to provoke over-reaction, one of the aims of outrages like the 9/11 attacks in the USA. Indeed, we have seen that SOE was very much aware of the potential negative impact of its actions, especially in terms of savage reprisals on the occupied population. Although SOE wanted to carry out sabotage and undermine the enemy's war effort, the occupiers' reaction could reduce the already ambivalent support for Resistance action. A Resistance army was needed, ready at the right time to impede German or Japanese defence against Allied invasion. Building up the will to resist, in a subjugated population, was a delicate process that could easily be set back by too much provocation or by premature action.

Selection

Telling the stories of a single group of men, especially since they had a specialist role, inevitably leads to an imbalanced and incomplete narrative of the whole organisation. A writer aiming to produce a comprehensive history would not start from there. But several excellent histories of the Intelligence Corps and, especially, SOE have been written. I have not aimed to compete with them. Rather, I have hoped to fill a gap left by these histories by focusing on the Field Security men who joined SOE in a relatively 'insignificant' capacity.

Even within the bounds I set for myself, I have had to be selective. For most of the war, about a hundred Field Security personnel served in SOE. Apart from them, many more members of the Intelligence Corps worked in the organisation. The more senior among them have their own biographies or autobiographies. This book tells the personal stories of just a few of what is already a small group.

These personal stories took our small group into a remarkable range of locations and activities. Nevertheless, the reach of SOE was global, so it is worth reflecting on what geographical areas this book leaves out. Through the constraints imposed by where members of this small group served, I have found little or no opportunity to cover SOE's activities in Norway, Yugoslavia, Greece, Russia, the USA or China, for example. The Note on Sources will lead the reader who wishes to explore these areas in the appropriate direction.

Pressure

One of the themes of this book has been the focus on the sense of security and precaution that the Field Security men tried to instil in agents. Yet it is difficult to imagine the psychological pressure on agents, who were in physical danger from the moment they set foot in their target country. It is not surprising that the habits of security that were essential to their survival were sometimes forgotten. It was tempting to speak English to comrades in a cafe or to keep an *aide-memoire* of codes, addresses or telephone numbers in a pocket. The lectures on security at Beaulieu and the tight-lipped example set by the Security Section could quickly be forgotten. Back in London, the country sections were under pressure too: working sixteen-hour days, six or seven days a week, and faced with decisions of life or death to be made in minutes. The absence of a security check in a garbled radio message called for a rapid judgement: was it a slip or a genuine warning?

Most arrests were the result of betrayal, but many were sparked by small errors. Mistakes were made, both in the field and at the various headquarters, and they cost lives. With hindsight, it is easy to pass judgement.

Arguments about the effectiveness of SOE persist today, with evidence being cited for opposing viewpoints. Whitehall rivalries led SOE to be beleaguered, secretive and defensive. As a result, resources and lives were wasted. Misconceptions about the willingness of subjugated peoples to rise up led to exaggerated claims of SOE's potential. As a result, expectations were dashed. Entire networks were infiltrated through sloppy security and effective enemy counter-insurgency. As a result, courageous agents were captured, tortured and executed.

Yet the purpose of this book has not been to examine these important issues, nor to describe the high-level decision-makers. Others have done this. Rather, I have tried – in the political and operational context – to tell the stories of a few individuals in humbler positions, who worked to keep SOE secure and therefore effective. Many of them played a more active role in operations, too, but all of them helped Churchill's secret creation to do its job.

Acknowledgements

Those who have commented on drafts of my text have generously given of their invaluable knowledge, saving me from many embarrassing slips and errors. Among them are Rod Bailey, Nick Fox, David Harrison, David Hewson, Steven McCormack, Paul McCue and Philip Towle. Fred Judge, an expert on the history of the Intelligence Corps, has not only shared his encyclopaedic knowledge; he has also made available sections of his comprehensive unpublished historical notes on the Field Security Sections.

Some of the above are members of the Yahoo Group on SOE, but other members who have been extremely helpful are David Armstrong, Hugh Bullock, David Blair, Rolf Dahlo, and David Foulk. In particular, Steven Kippax has made it a labour of love to digitise and collate hundreds of SOE-related files at The National Archives. Without his rich collection, I would have spent many more days than I did, travelling to Kew and consulting the physical files. At other archives, Joyce Hutton of the Military Intelligence Museum and the Research Room staff at the Imperial War Museum have gone out of their way to support my efforts.

James Morgan has been long-suffering and patient as we have gone through many late-night email exchanges to refine the cover designs and the interior illustrations. I have been privileged to benefit from his artistic input. The final result has also been much improved by Mark Swift's painstaking copy-editing.

Family members and relatives of some of the subjects of this book have been very helpful. Wendy Martyn helped me to get in touch with Teddy Bisset's family. Jonathan Rée fact-checked the section on his father Harry and sent me a memoir from his family's archives.

Kim Spencer has recounted reminiscences of his father and searched out photographs. Richard Windred entrusted me with some irreplaceable family documents, including his mother's precious diaries.

The greatest contribution of my own family has been their encouragement. In particular, my wife Ingrid knows all about writing a book and has kept me alive, encouraged my progress when I hit the buffers and given me patient support. I couldn't have done it without her!

Dramatis Personae

The following incomplete list of the individuals named in this book shows a representative rank and the main contexts in which they appear in the book, but with a particular focus on those who were members of SOE's Field Security Sections. No attempt is made to describe any individual's full career.

Flight Officer Vera Atkins	F Section Intelligence Officer, post-war investigator.
Major Arthur Baird	63 FSS, Cairo Italy.
Sergeant 'Dickie' Bell	65/30 FSS NW Europe.
Captain Teddy Bisset	64 FSS, Dieppe Raid, F Section, *Mission Tilleul*, killed September 1944.
Winfred Bisset (née Marshall)	Pianist and journalist from Western Australia.
Lieutenant Frank Boyall	65 FSS, PWE Italian group to India.
Colonel Maurice Buckmaster	F Section head.
Captain Henri Déricourt	Air-landing ops organiser, double agent.
Captain Frank Donaldson	65 FSS, Dieppe Raid, 300 FSS Italy.
Major General 'Wild Bill' Donovan	OSS Director.
Sergeant James Edgar	63 FSS, *Mission Tilleul* radio operator.
Major Aonghais Fyffe	Inverlair 'cooler', Thame Park, Bayswater Security Section, ME42.
Lieutenant Stuart Gardiner	FS duties, agent in Belgium.
Major-General Colin Gubbins	SOE Director of Training and Operations and later head.
Sergeant George Harker	63 FSS, PWE, Dutch Section radio operator.
Captain Peter Harratt	Dieppe Raid.
Sergeant Antoni Hartog	FS duties, STS 2, (Bonzos), ME 42.
Lieutenant Arthur Hodson	FS duties, conducting officer for French.

Captain Geoffrey Holland	63 FSS, FSO 65 FSS, No 1 SF Italy.
Major Peter Lee	Security Section, *Massingham*, Algiers, 300 FSS Italy.
Lieutenant Ken Macalister	64 FSS, F Section agent, executed Buchenwald September 1944.
Major Ian Mackenzie	*Mission Tilleul* medical officer.
Lieutenant Fred Morris	63 FSS, *Massingham* Algiers, 300 FSS Italy.
Major Norman Mott	64 FSS, Security Section, SOE wind-down.
Major John Oughton	64 FSS, STS 43, *Brandon* mission, *Massingham* Algiers, No 4 SFU, Australia.
Major Frank Pickering	64 FSS, RVPS, Op *Clowder* Slovenia.
Major Jacques Vaillant de Guélis	F Section, AMF Section Algiers, *Mission Tilleul*, died after motor accident 1945.
Regimental Sergeant Major Eric 'Farmer' Rée	65 FSS, *Massingham* Algiers, died November 1943.
Captain Harry Rée	FS duties, F Section agent.
Captain Anelyf Rees	64 FSS, FSO 64 Section, Security Section.
Captain Frank Pickering	64 FSS, RVPS interrogation, Op *Clowder* Croatia.
Captain Frank Pickersgill	Canadian agent, executed Buchenwald September 1944.
Sergeant Arthur Ronnfeldt	FS duties, Beaulieu, ME24 safe house.
Flight Lieutenant André Simon	*Mission Tilleul* air operations.
Major Robert Searle	63 FSS, F Section, *Massingham* Algiers training, Centre 20 Rambouillet.
Commander John Senter	SOE Director of Security.
Captain Gilbert Smith	64 FSS, Camberley Reception Depot, Station IX Welwyn, X Section.
Captain Geoffrey Spencer	FSO, X Section.
Captain Robert Stebbing-Allen	FS duties, Cairo, F133 Italy.
Captain Brian Walmsley	FSO 63 FSS, Photographic Section, DF Section Algiers and Seville.
Lieutenant-Colonel Dick Warden	63 FSS, Beaulieu, Bayswater Special Section.
Captain George Windred	Australian, 65 FSS, Oriental Mission Malaya and Thailand.
Gwendoline Windred	Australian pianist.
Pearl Witherington	F Section agent.

Glossary

The following list unpacks a selection of SOE-related terms and abbreviations, not all of which are necessarily abbreviated, or even appear, in this book.

Abwehr	German military intelligence
AMF	SOE Section operating into France from North Africa
AS	*Armée secrète*
BBC	British Broadcasting Corporation
BEF	British Expeditionary Force (1940)
Bigot	Security clearance caveat to protect *Overlord*
BSC	British Security Cooperation (New York)
BSS	Bayswater Security Section
Beaulieu	Base of SOE 'Finishing Schools'
BLO	British Liaison Officer (e.g. with Yugoslavian partisans)
C	Head of Secret Intelligence Service
CD	Executive Director of Special Operations Executive
D/F	[Head of] SOE Section for clandestine escape
DGER	*Direction générale des Études et Recherches*
DZ	Dropping Zone
EH	Electra House (propaganda organisation)
EMFFI	*État-Major des Forces Françaises de l'Intérieur*
EU/P	[Head of] SOE Section for Poles in France
F	[Head of] SOE (Independent) French Section
FANY	First Aid Nursing Yeomanry
FFI	*Forces Françaises de l'Intérieur*
FO	Foreign Office
Force 133	SOE Balkans
Force 136	SOE Far East
FTP	*Francs-Tireurs et Partisans*

FSS, FSO	Field Security Section/Officer
ISLD	Inter-Services Liaison Department (cover for SIS)
ISRB	Inter-Services Research Bureau (cover for SOE)
J	[Head of] SOE Italian Section
Jedburgh	Three-man teams for post-invasion liaison with Resistance
LZ	Landing zone
Maryland	Code name for No 1 Special Force
Massingham	Code name for SOE North Africa base near Algiers
Maquis	Guerrilla units, rural France (members were *maquisards*)
ME24	Military Establishment 24, Paris Mission 1944
ME42	Military Establishment 42, SOE presence in Germany 1945
MEW	Ministry of Economic Warfare
MI5	Security Service
MI6	Secret Intelligence Service
MI9	War Office section assisting escaping airmen and POWs
MI(R)	Military Intelligence (Research)
MO1(SP)	SOE cover name, especially with military
MOI	Ministry of Information
Musgrave	SOE Section tasked with planning for support of *Overlord*
N	[Head of] SOE Netherlands Section
NCO	Non-commissioned Officer
No I SF	No I Special Force, SOE formation in Italy
OM	Oriental Mission, Singapore 1941-42
OSS	[United States] Office of Strategic Services
OSS/SI	Intelligence element of OSS
OSS/SO	Special operations element of OSS
Overlord	Allied invasion of northwest Europe, June 1944
PE	Plastic explosive
POW	Prisoner-of-War
PWE	Political Warfare Executive
RF	[Head of] SOE Gaullist/Free French Section
RAF	Royal Air Force
RN	Royal Navy
RVPS	Royal Victoria Patriotic Schools (alien clearing centre)
S	[Head of] SOE Scandinavian Section

SAS	Special Air Service
SD	*Sicherheitsdienst* (Security Service)
Section D	(pre-SOE) SIS sabotage section
SF	Special Forces
SF Det	Special Forces Detachment liaising with Army/Army Group HQ
SFHQ	Special Forces Headquarters
SHAEF	Supreme Headquarters Allied Expeditionary Force
SIS	Secret Intelligence Service (MI6)
SOI	Special Operations 1 – propaganda (became part of PWE)
SO2	Special Operations 2 – operations (became SOE)
SO3	Special Operations 3 – planning (ceased to exist as separate entity)
SOE	Special Operations Executive
SOE/SO	British/American combined predecessor of SFHQ.
SOM	Special Operations (Mediterranean)
SPOC	Combined SOE/OSS Special Projects Operations Centre at *Massingham* for special operations in southern France
SSRF	Small-scale Raiding Force
STS	Special Training School
T	[Head of] SOE Belgian Section
Ultra	Intelligence product of Bletchley Park codebreaking
USAAF	United States Army Air Forces
W/T	Wireless telegraphy
X	[Head of] SOE German Section

Note on Sources

I have assembled this book using what intelligence historian Professor Christopher Andrew has called the 'Lego method'. In doing so I have used a wide range of primary and secondary sources, but I have not been aiming to produce an academic history. I have therefore generally only provided references where I am quoting directly from published works or primary sources.

Hundreds of books have been written about the SOE and a few about the Intelligence Corps, and many of these have provided me with valuable background, but I have also gone to the primary material such as the files at the National Archives (TNA) in Kew and the collections of the Imperial War Museum. Those SOE files that survived the 1946 fire at Baker Street have progressively been opened up to researchers in the National Archives since William Waldegrave's 1993 Open Government Initiative. That said, there are plenty of areas where the sources simply do not exist. One example is the *Massingham* base outside Algiers. For good security reasons, Douglas Dodds-Parker and his colleagues burned the files when they closed down the base, so researchers have had to find indirect ways of unearthing what information they can.

In the following sections, I divide sources into primary and secondary material, bur within those two categories I broadly follow the chapter sequence of the book. I mention a resource only for the first chapter in which it is relevant. At TNA, in addition to the files noted below, I have accessed the personal files of many of the individual members of SOE. At the Imperial War Museum, the proceedings of the major conference run by the Museum in 1998, entitled *Special Operations Executive: a New Instrument of War*, captured the voices of several then surviving members of the organisation. Other oral history interviews, lectures and personal papers are mentioned below.

Archives and Oral Histories

Chapter 1

TNA WO 167/1384	24 FSS Field Returns Dec 1939 – Oct 1940
TNA HS 6/354	*Operation Hangman*
TNA HS 6/367	*Mission Tilleul*
TNA HS 6/530	*Jedburgh* Team *James* Report
TNA HS 9/355/2, 9/356	Cecile Pearl Cornioley
IWM 11934	Private Papers of Miss W B Marshall

Chapter 2

TNA HS 8/832	History of Security Section/Personnel
TNA HS7/222	Survey of Global Activities November 1941
IWM 23100	Oral History – Fyffe
IWM 6808	Oral History – Heath
IWM 7493	Oral History – Lee

Chapter 3

TNA HS 7/31	History of Security Section, FSP, penetration
TNA HS7/111	History of Oriental Mission and SOE in Far East
TNA HS 1/207	Oriental Mission History
TNA WO 93/911	Irregular Activities Far East 1940-42
TNA HS 6/886	Italian recruits from US
TNA WO 208/3039	Mazzini Mission: reports and correspondence
TNA FO 939/373	India: PW mission; Mazzini Society
IWM 2929	Private Papers of Mrs U M Streatfeild
IWM 2927	Private Papers of E W Deane
IWM 2049	Private Papers of A A Gentry
IWM 15167	Private Papers of Flight Lieutenant P H Taggart
Gwen Windred	Personal correspondence and diaries 1935-1946 (by kind permission of Richard Windred)
Talk by Dr Donald P LaTourette	The Australasian Record, Vol 47, No 4, Warburton, Victoria, 25th January 1943.

Chapter 4

TNA KV 4/171	MI5 report on SOE training
TNA HS 9/307/3	Marie Christine Chilver (*Fifi*)
IWM 18559	Oral history – Ferrier
IWM 10446	Oral history – Poirier
IWM 18593	Oral history – panel on RAF special operations
IWM 18594	Oral history – panel on SOE in France
IWM 4843	Oral History – Abbott

Chapter 5

IWM 8720, 13064	Oral History – Rée

Chapter 6

TNA HS 3/169	Middle East Mission Cairo Org 1941-2
TNA HS 3/170	Middle East Mission Cairo 1943
TNA HS 7/169	*Massingham* Mission History
TNA HS 8/885	Italy- Security reports
TNA HS 6/875	Italy- Security Intelligence Panel Policy
TNA HS 7/58	SOE Activities in Italy1941-45
TNA WO 204	300 FSS Italy
TNA HS 7/60	Italy April 1945

Chapter 7

TNA HS 6/705-708	SOE Paris Mission
TNA HS 7/145-7	German Section History
TNA HS 8/883	Operations into Germany- *Bonzos*
TNA HS/8/332	SOE Directives and SF Detachment Reports
TNA HS 6/680	*Operation Branston*
TNA FO 898/354	Breaking German will to resist, *Op Periwig*
IWM 26504	Private papers of Captain G A D Spencer
IWM 16378	64 and 65 FSS, SOE, 1944-45

Books, Theses and Articles

The publications mentioned here represent a small selection that have been useful to my research. I have tended to prefer official histories and authentic first-hand accounts rather than sometimes fanciful secondary sources.

Chapter 1

Personal experience of service in a Field Security Section in the British Expeditionary Force was recounted in the contemporary 1940 book by Captain Sir Basil Bartlett (*My First War: an Army Officer's journal for May 1940: through Belgium to Dunkirk*, Basil Sir Bartlett, 1940). William Mackenzie's official SOE history (*The Secret History of SOE: the Special Operations Executive, 1940-1945*, W J M Mackenzie, 2000), once classified and only available to approved 'genuine' historians, was declassified and published in 2000. It remains a valuable resource, especially with M R D Foot's Foreword and notes.

Foot's own prodigious output of knowledge on SOE is also invaluable, particularly his detailed assessments of SOE's work in France (*SOE in France: an account of the work of the British special operations executive in France 1940-1944*, M R D Foot, 2006) and the Low Countries (*SOE in the Low Countries*, M R D Foot, 2001), and his broader-brush history of SOE (*SOE: an outline history of the Special Operations Executive 1940-1946*, M R D Foot, 2008). His personal memoir is more an autobiography, but has some interesting comments about SOE and the other secret organisations (*Memories of an SOE Historian*, M R D Foot, 2008).

David Stafford, with limited access to archives at the time, analysed the political context and impact of SOE (*Britain and European Resistance, 1940-1945: a survey of the Special Operations Executive, with documents*, David Stafford, 1980), as well as writing a companion volume to a television series about SOE (*Secret Agent: the true story of the Special Operations Executive*, David Stafford, 2000). A more recent popular history of SOE is by Giles Milton (*Churchill's Ministry of Ungentlemanly Warfare: the mavericks who plotted Hitler's defeat*, Giles Milton, 2017).

Three personal memoirs of working in SOE, particularly in London, are by Bickham Sweet-Escott (*Baker Street Irregular*, Bickham Sweet-Escott, 1965), Douglas Dodds-Parker (*Setting Europe Ablaze: some account of ungentlemanly warfare*, Douglas Dodds-Parker, 1983) and John Beevor (*SOE: recollections and reflections 1940-1945*, John G Beevor, 1981). The more irreverent, and often very entertaining, memoir of an SOE cryptographer (*Between Silk and Cyanide: a codemaker's story 1941-1945*, Leo Marks, 2008) captures the SOE culture and many of its personalities. On the security aspects of SOE, Christopher Murphy's detailed treatment of the Security Section is more academically rigorous than the present book, focusing particularly on the relationship with MI5 (*Security and Special Operations: SOE and MI5 during the Second World War*, Christopher J Murphy, 2006).

Thousands of books are in print on the Second World War, but two very readable ones by Max Hastings cover respectively the general context of the war and the place of SOE in clandestine affairs (*All Hell Let Loose: the world at war 1939-45*, Max Hastings, 2011; *The Secret War: spies, codes and guerrillas, 1939-1945*, Max Hastings, 2015). Similarly accessible, the first part of Ian Kershaw's ambitious history of the 20th century (*To Hell and Back: Europe, 1914-1949*, Ian Kershaw, 2015) places the Second World War in the overall context of the growth of authoritarianism in Europe.

The number of books on the controversial Dieppe Raid is also vast, but most are concerned with higher-level planning, inter-Allied politics and the possibility of German foreknowledge. Information on the SOE role in the raid is much more difficult to unearth. It is briefly covered in Foot's SOE in France and Hugh Henry's unpublished PhD thesis on the operation (*The Planning, Intelligence, Execution and Aftermath of the Dieppe raid, 19 August 1942*, Hugh G Henry, 1996).

Max Hastings appears here yet again, with his book on the harassment of the 2nd SS Panzer Division by the French Resistance (*Das Reich: the march of the 2nd SS Panzer Division through France, June 1944*, Max Hastings, 2009). Also, an authentic book on the Resistance in the Corrèze (*L'Armée Secrète en Haute-Corrèze 1942-1944*, Louis Le Moigne and Marcel Barbanceys, 1993), focusing on the AS, was obtained at the *Musée Départemental de la Résistance 'Henri Queuille'* in Neuvic.

Peter Dixon

Chapter 2

Peter Wilkinson and Joan Bright Astley's biography of Colin Gubbins has a focus on his role in SOE, as the title suggests, but includes much more (*Gubbins and SOE*, Peter Wilkinson and Joan Bright Astley, 1993). Malcolm Atkin's recent history of the Auxiliary Units (*Fighting Nazi Occupation: British resistance 1939-1945*, Malcolm Atkin, 2015) covers the planned resistance to a potential German invasion of Britain, with which Gubbins was intimately involved.

Tom Keene covers the Whitehall battles that threatened SOE's existence throughout the war (*Cloak of Enemies: Churchill's SOE, enemies at home and the 'Cockleshell heroes'*, Tom Keene, 2012). Similarly, Paddy Ashdown's narrative history of the Combined Operations canoe raid on Bordeaux, *Operation Frankton*, (*A Brilliant Little Operation: the cockleshell heroes and the most courageous raid of WW2*, Paddy Ashdown, 2012) exposes the inter-agency rivalries and secrecy that cost many lives, while he focuses more specifically on SOE in his look at the battle of wits between agents and counter-intelligence officers (*Game of Spies: the secret agent, the traitor and the Nazi, Bordeaux 1942-1944*, Paddy Ashdown, 2016).

Anthony Clayton's comprehensive history of the Intelligence Corps (*Forearmed: a history of the Intelligence Corps*, Anthony Clayton, 1993) and Nicholas Van der Bijl's more recent equivalent (*Sharing the Secret: the history of the Intelligence Corps 1940-2010*, Nicholas Van der Bijl, 2013) are both important resources. In addition, reminiscences of service in (non-SOE) Field Security Sections are in the Intelligence Corps Association's journal *Rose & Laurel*.

Chapter 3

David Garnett has written an official history of the Political Warfare Executive 1939-1945 (*The Secret History of PWE: the Political Warfare Executive, 1939-1945*, David Garnett, 2002)., but more detail on the Italian-Americans' 'deployment' to India is in a book chapter by Kent Fedorowich (*The Mazzini Society and Political Warfare among Italian POWs in India, 1941–1943*, Kent Fedorowich, in 'Toughs and thugs':

208

the politics and strategy of clandestine war: Special Operation Executive, 1940-1946, edited by Neville Wylie, 2007).

Charles Cruickshank's official history of SOE's Far Eastern role (SOE in the Far East, Charles Greig Cruickshank, 1983) helps to unearth what little can be learned about George Windred's exploits in Siam, while the pre-war diplomatic background is covered by Nicholas Tarling (Britain, Southeast Asia and the Onset of the Pacific War, Nicholas Tarling, 1996). General information on undercover operations in the region is to be found in books by Richard Aldrich (Intelligence and the War against Japan: Britain, America and the politics of secret service, Richard J Aldrich, 2000). and, specifically on Thailand, E. Bruce Reynolds (Thailand's Secret War: the Free Thai, OSS and SOE during World War II, E Bruce Reynolds, 2005) and Andrew Gilchrist (Bangkok Top Secret: being the experiences of a British Officer in the Siam Country Section of Force 136, Sir Andrew Gilchrist, 1970). A helpful journal article by Richard Aldrich (A Question of Expediency: Britain, the United States and Thailand, 1941–42, Richard J Aldrich, 2009) shows how US-UK rivalry over the post-war order played out in Thailand.

Chapter 4

Derwin Gregory's unpublished PhD thesis is a comprehensive study of SOE's physical infrastructure in the UK (Built to Resist: an assessment of the Special Operations Executive's infrastructure in the United Kingdom during the Second World War, 1940-1946, Derwin Gregory, 2015). On the Finishing Schools, local historian Cyril Cunningham's book on Beaulieu was helpful (Beaulieu: the finishing school for secret agents 1941-1945, Cyril Cunningham, 1998). Fred Judge has generously provided extracts from his unpublished history of all Field Security Sections, providing helpful data on those that were part of SOE.

The diaries of Guy Liddell, MI5's chief of counter-intelligence, edited by Nigel West (The Guy Liddell Diaries: MI5's director of counter-espionage in World War II, Guy Maynard Liddell and Nigel West, 2009), give interesting insights on SOE's security, seen from the outside. Liddell's diaries also focus on the handling of double agents during the war, under the XX system described by John Masterman (*The Double-Cross System in the War of 1939-1945*, J C Masterman, 1979) and popularised by Ben Macintyre (*Double Cross: the true story of the D-day spies*, Ben Macintyre, 2012). Christopher Murphy, mentioned above, devotes a chapter to the investigation of *Unternehmen Nordpol* by MI5 and SOE's Security Section.

Chapter 5

I have drawn together Ken Macalister's and Harry Rée's stories from archive material. However, they appear in many of the accounts of SOE in France. More specifically, Jonathan Vance's biography of Macalister and his compatriot circuit organiser Frank Pickersgill (*Unlikely Soldiers: how two Canadians fought the secret war against Nazi occupation*, Jonathan F Vance, 2008) gives a comprehensive account of his life, whereas Edward Cookridge's books on SOE in general and on three of its agents include Rée's exploits (*Inside SOE: the story of special operations in Western Europe, 1940-45*, Edward H Cookridge, 1966, *They Came from the Sky*, Edward H Cookridge, 1976).

SOE's maritime raids and sea transport to and from occupied territory were comprehensively covered by Brooks Richards in *Secret Flotillas*, first published in 1996 (*Secret Flotillas, vol 1: Clandestine Sea Operations to Brittany, 1940-1944*, Brooks Richards, 2004). The airborne equivalent is Hugh Verity's 1978 book (*We Landed by Moonlight: secret RAF landings in France, 1940-1944*, Hugh Verity, 1995).

Alongside M R D Foot's seminal history of SOE's activities in France, mentioned above, a recent book by Robert Gildea (*Fighters in the Shadows: a New History of the French Resistance*, Robert Gildea, 2015) attempts to balance some of the myths that have been cultivated about the French Resistance.

Chapter 6

The atmosphere in Cairo is amply described in a chapter of Bickham Sweet-Escott's book, mentioned above. Martin Thomas and T C Wales have both written on Anglo-American cooperation at Massingham in the wider political context (*The Massingham Mission: SOE in French North Africa, 1941–1944*, Martin Thomas, 1996, *The 'Massingham' Mission and the Secret 'Special Relationship': cooperation and rivalry between the Anglo-American clandestine services in French North Africa, November 1942–May 1943*, T C Wales, 2005). Italy's surrender is covered in a very early account (*Now it Can be Told*, James Gleeson and Tom Waldron, 1951), whereas the official histories of SOE in Italy, before and after the Allied invasion respectively, are by Roderick Bailey and David Stafford (*Mission Accomplished: SOE and Italy 1943-1945*, David Stafford, 2011; *Target Italy: the secret war against Mussolini, 1940-1943*, Roderick Bailey, 2014).

Chapter 7

A wealth of literature exists about the birth and activities of the OSS, primarily as the forerunner of the Central Intelligence Agency, and the OSS War Report has long been declassified (*War Report of the Office of Strategic Services, Vol 1 and 2*, 1947). More specifically, David Stafford and Lynn Hodgson have both written about the training facility, STS 103, popularised as Camp X (*Camp X: SOE and the American connection*, David Stafford, 1986; *Inside Camp X*, Lynn-Philip Hodgson, 1999). The development and implementation of the *Jedburgh* concept is described from an American viewpoint by Wyman Irwin (*A Special Force: origin and development of the Jedburgh project in support of Operation Overlord*, Wyman W Irwin, 1991). Sarah Helm's biography of Vera Atkins covers her post-war investigations in Germany (*A Life in Secrets: the story of Vera Atkins and the lost agents of SOE*, Sarah Helm, 2005).

Other Resources for Further Research

Several blog posts on the **National Archives** website (http://blog.nationalarchives.gov.uk/) expand on specific aspects of SOE's history, and you can find relevant files through their user-friendly Discovery search engine. The start point for browsing SOE files is http://discovery.nationalarchives.gov.uk/details/r/C153, but searching may be easier. A minority of files are downloadable for a modest fee, but for most you have to visit the modern archive facilities at Kew, to the west of London. Register in advance for a free Reader's Ticket and place an online order before your visit for the files you would like to peruse.

Some informational articles on the **Imperial War Museum** website (https://www.iwm.org.uk/history) may be relevant, but it too has a helpful search facility for its extensive collections. Many images can be viewed on the site and you can listen online to hours of oral history interviews. When I last looked, a search on 'Special Operations Executive' yielded 552 recordings, most of which can be streamed to your computer.

That said, the reader who wishes to look further into SOE cannot do better than starting with two excellent websites. The first is **Nigel Perrin**'s site (www.nigelperrin.com), which lists and comments on over 100 books and two dozen DVDs on the subject, most with links to a purchase. The second is the **Secret WW2 Learning Network,** an educational charity that aims to create greater public awareness of the contributions and experiences of the men and women who took part during the Second World War in Allied special operations, intelligence gathering and resistance – principally, but not exclusively, in Britain and France (www.secret-ww2.net).

Regarding the Intelligence Corps, the website of the Military Intelligence Museum at Chicksands, Bedfordshire, is worth a visit (www.militaryintelligencemuseum.org/), and a physical visit to the Museum and Archives can be arranged. On the Second World War more generally, there are several relevant websites, many with sections devoted to SOE or other clandestine organisations; they include www.ww2talk.com, which covers all aspects of the 1939-45 war but has a 'Top Secret' section and special forces unit histories. Whatever the subject of your query, there is probably an expert who can answer it.

For a more intimate impression of SOE, many of the locations mentioned in this book can easily be found. You can visit Beaulieu. You can stay at Arisaig House or St Ermin's Hotel. You can walk down Baker Street and stand outside Orchard Court. Perhaps, though, you can never fully recapture the atmosphere of the secret world of the Special Operations Executive.

List of Images

Index

Bibliography

Aldrich, Richard J. 2000. *Intelligence and the War against Japan: Britain, America and the politics of secret service.* Cambridge ; New York: Cambridge University Press.

Aldrich, Richard J. 2009. "A Question of Expediency: Britain, the United States and Thailand, 1941–42." *Journal of Southeast Asian Studies* 19 (2):209-244.

Ashdown, Paddy. 2012. *A Brilliant Little Operation: the cockleshell heroes and the most courageous raid of WW2.* London: Aurum.

Ashdown, Paddy. 2016. *Game of Spies: the secret agent, the traitor and the Nazi, Bordeaux 1942-1944.*

Atkin, Malcolm. 2015. *Fighting Nazi Occupation: British resistance 1939-1945.*

Bailey, Roderick. 2014. *Target Italy: the secret war against Mussolini, 1940-1943.*

Bartlett, Basil Sir. 1940. *My First War: An Army Officer's journal for May, 1940: through Belgium to Dunkirk.* [S.l.]: Chatto & Windus.

Beevor, John G. 1981. *SOE: recollections and reflections 1940-1945.* London: Bodley Head.

Clayton, Anthony. 1993. *Forearmed: a history of the Intelligence Corps.* London: Brassey's (UK).

Cookridge, Edward Henry. 1966. *Inside SOE: The story of special operations in Western Europe, 1940-45.* London: Arthur Barker.

Cookridge, Edward Henry. 1976. *They Came from the Sky.* London: Corgi.

Costello, John. 1988. *Mask of Treachery.* London: Collins.

Cruickshank, Charles Greig. 1983. *SOE in the Far East.* Oxford: Oxford University Press.

Cunningham, Cyril. 1998. *Beaulieu: the finishing school for secret agents 1941-1945.* London: Leo Cooper.

Dixon, Ingrid. 2016. *The Bride's Trunk: a story of war and reconciliation.* Cloudshill Press.

Dodds-Parker, Douglas. 1983. *Setting Europe Ablaze : some account of ungentlemanly warfare.* Windlesham, Surrey: Springwood Books.

Fedorowich, Kent. 2007. "The Mazzini Society and Political Warfare among Italian POWs in India, 1941–1943." In *'Toughs and thugs': The politics and strategy of clandestine war : Special Operation Executive, 1940-1946*, edited by Neville Wylie. London: Routledge.

Foot, M R D. 2001. *SOE in the Low Countries*. London: St Ermin's.

Foot, M R D. 2006. *SOE in France: an account of the work of the British special operations executive in France 1940-1944*. [S.l.] : HMSO, 1966 (1976).

Foot, M R D. 2008. *Memories of an SOE Historian*. Barnsley: Pen & Sword Military.

Foot, M R D. 2008. *SOE: an outline history of the Special Operations Executive 1940-1946*. London: Folio Society.

Garnett, David. 2002. *The Secret History of PWE: the Political Warfare Executive, 1939-1945*. London: St Ermin's.

Gilchrist, Andrew Sir. 1970. *Bangkok Top Secret: being the experiences of a British Officer in the Siam Country Section of Force 136*, London: Hutchinson.

Gildea, Robert. 2015. *Fighters in the Shadows : a New Hstory of the French Resistance*.

Gleeson, James, and Tom Waldron. 1951. *Now it Can be Told*. [S.l.]: Paul Elek.

Gregory, Derwin. 2015. "Built to Resist: An assessment of the Special Operations Executive's infrastructure in the United Kingdom during the Second World War, 1940-1946." PhD, University of East Anglia.

Gubbins, Colin. 1939. The Art of Guerrilla Warfare. London.

Hastings, Max. 2009. *Das Reich: the march of the 2nd SS Panzer Division through France, June 1944*. London: Pan.

Hastings, Max. 2011. *All Hell Let Loose: the world at war 1939-45*. London: HarperPress.

Hastings, Max. 2015. *The Secret War: spies, codes and guerrillas, 1939-1945*.

Helm, Sarah. 2005. *A Life in Secrets: the story of Vera Atkins and the lost agents of SOE*. London: Little, Brown.

Henry, Hugh G. 1996. "The Planning, Intelligence, Execution and Aftermath of the Dieppe raid, 19 August 1942." PhD, University of Cambridge.

Hodgson, Lynn-Philip. 1999. *Inside Camp X*. Oakville, Ont., Canada, L.P. Hodgson.

Irwin, Wyman W. 1991. *A Special Force: Origin and development of the Jedburgh project in support of Operation.*

Keene, Tom. 2012. *Cloak of Enemies: Churchill's SOE, enemies at home and the 'Cockleshell heroes'.* Stroud: Spellmount.

Kershaw, Ian. 2015. *To Hell and Back: Europe, 1914-1949.*

Le Moigne, Louis, and Marcel Barbanceys. 1993. *L'Armée Secrète en Haute-Corrèze 1942-1944.* Ussel.

Liddell, Guy Maynard, and Nigel West. 2009. *The Guy Liddell Diaries: MI5's director of counter-espionage in World War II.* London: Routledge.

Macintyre, Ben. 2012. *Double Cross: the true story of the D-day spies.* New York: Crown.

Mackenzie, W J M. 2000. *The Secret History of SOE: the Special Operations Executive, 1940-1945.* London: St Ermin's.

Marks, Leo. 2008. *Between Silk and Cyanide: a codemaker's story 1941-1945.* Stroud: History Press.

Masterman, J C. 1979. *The Double-Cross System in the War of 1939-1945.* London: Panther.

Milton, Giles. 2017. *Churchill's Ministry of Ungentlemanly Warfare: the mavericks who plotted Hitler's defeat.* New York: Picador.

Muggeridge, Malcolm. 1973. *Chronicles of Wasted Time, vol. 2: The Infernal Grove.* [S.l.]: Collins.

Murphy, Christopher J. 2006. *Security and Special Operations : SOE and MI5 during the Second World War.* Basingstoke: Palgrave Macmillan.

Reynolds, E Bruce. 2005. *Thailand's Secret War : the Free Thai, OSS and SOE during World War II.* Cambridge: Cambridge University Press.

Richards, Brooks. 2004. *Secret Flotillas, vol 1: Clandestine Sea Operations to Brittany, 1940-1944.* London: Whitehall History Publishing in association with Frank Cass.

Stafford, David. 1980. *Britain and European Resistance, 1940-1945: a survey of the Special Operations Executive, with documents.* Toronto: University of Toronto Press.

Stafford, David. 1986. *Camp X: SOE and the American connection.* [Harmondsworth]: Viking, 1987.

Stafford, David. 2000. *Secret Agent: the true story of the Special Operations Executive.* London: BBC.

Stafford, David. 2011. *Mission Accomplished: SOE and Italy 1943-1945*. London: Bodley Head.

Suttill, Francis J. 2014. *Shadows in the Fog: the true story of Major Suttill and the Prosper French Resistance network*. History Press.

Suttill, Francis J, and M R D Foot. 2011. "SOE's 'Prosper' Disaster of 1943." *Intelligence and National Security* 26 (1):99-105.

Sweet-Escott, Bickham. 1965. *Baker Street Irregular*. London,: Methuen.

Tarling, Nicholas. 1996. *Britain, Southeast Asia and the Onset of the Pacific War*. Cambridge England ; New York, NY, USA, Cambridge University Press.

Thomas, Martin. 1996. "The Massingham Mission: SOE in French North Africa, 1941–1944." *Intelligence and National Security* 11 (4):696-721.

Van der Bijl, Nicholas. 2013. *Sharing the Secret: the history of the Intelligence Corps 1940-2010*. Pen & Sword Military.

Vance, Jonathan Franklin William. 2008. *Unlikely Soldiers: how two Canadians fought the secret war against Nazi occupation*. Toronto: HarperCollins Publishers.

Verity, Hugh. 1995. *We Landed by Moonlight: secret RAF landings in France, 1940-1944*. Wilmslow: Air Data.

Wales, T C. 2005. "The 'Massingham' Mission and the Secret 'Special Relationship': Cooperation and Rivalry between the Anglo-American Clandestine Services in French North Africa, November 1942–May 1943." *Intelligence and National Security* 20 (1):44-71.

War Report of the Office of Strategic Services, Vol 1 and 2. 1947. Washington DC: Office of the Assistant Secretary of War.

Wilkinson, Peter, and Joan Bright Astley. 1993. *Gubbins and SOE*. Barnsley: Pen & Sword Military, 2010.

About the Author

Dr Peter Dixon is a researcher, author and lecturer. He served over 30 years as a Royal Air Force pilot and spent the next decade leading the charity Concordis International in its conflict resolution work in Sudan and other divided societies. He completed his doctoral research at the University of Cambridge in 2015, studying outside intervention in civil wars. His writing has included *Amazon Task Force*, the story of a medical expedition in the Peruvian Amazon, and *Peacemakers: Building stability in a complex world*.

He and his wife Ingrid, also an author, live in Gloucestershire. They have two adult children and five grandchildren.

Made in the USA
Middletown, DE
20 November 2018